CW00746993

GOOD WITH NUMBERS

FRANK CRONIN AND
THE BINGO BOOM

Nigel Watson

First published 2011 in Great Britain by
St Matthew's Press
10 St Matthew's Terrace, Leyburn, North Yorkshire DL8 5EL

Copyright © Nigel Watson 2011

ISBN 978-0-9565452-1-3

All rights reserved. No part of this publication may be reproduced, stored or introduced into a retrieval system or transmitted in any form or by any means, electronic, mechanical, photocopying, recording or otherwise, without the prior written permission of the publisher of this book.

Design and artwork by Brian Glanfield CREATIVE DESIGN
Hillside, Grassgill, West Witton, North Yorkshire DL8 4LY

Printed and bound by Butler Tanner & Dennis Ltd, Caxton Road, Frome, Somerset BA11 1NF

CONTENTS

Acknowledgements

Bingo is a game which has brought pleasure to countless millions and Frank Cronin is one of the men who made this possible. But this book, suggested by Phil Cronin and his brothers, is also about Frank Cronin the family man whose roots remain in Sunderland, the city of his birth. I have enjoyed the pleasure of talking to Frank over many hours about his life and much appreciate the time he gave me. I would also like to thank all those members of his family, friends and business colleagues who helped me to piece together the story of his life – Fr Jim Cronin, Stephen Cronin, Paul Cronin, Phil Cronin, Paddy Cronin, Tom Clark, Ray Smith, Ray Brown, Jim and Madge Johnson, Brian Walsh, Linda Holden, Pat Bevis and Neil and Pam Wright. Much of the detail for the background to the game of bingo and its modern development was drawn from Carolyn Downs, A Brief History of Bingo, (September 2008), which can be viewed on playingbingo.co.uk, as well as numerous press articles.

Nigel Watson
Winter 2010-11

Foreword

We felt that Dad's story was one worth telling, even if only for family and friends. Stephen, Paul, Paddy and myself all have our own personal stories about Dad and you can find some of these in the book. This is an extraordinary story about a remarkable man and the business he built. Throughout my time both inside and outside the company I have never met anyone who comes close to Dad in matching his entrepreneurial flair, his unwavering self-belief, and his appreciation of his responsibility as an employer. Although he and I have quarrelled many times about work, I personally learnt so much from him and he is a very hard act to follow. As a teenager I was allowed to sit in his office and watch him work, usually before or after a game of squash. With three phones on his desk, he and his secretary Pat used to juggle calls with the queue of people waiting at the door. Switching from one issue to another Dad always had something to contribute, a new way of looking at things, a new angle and a confidence that rubbed off on others. Everything was possible, there had to be a way of solving a problem or satisfying a customer, we just had to figure it out. His most powerful lesson is one he says he learnt from his own Dad, to treat everyone with respect whoever they were. To me he appears more proud of the people he has employed throughout his career than anything else, proud of the contribution he was able to make but also proud of the great work done by the people at Edward Thompson.

We hope you enjoy the story and if you were part of it, all of us, including Dad, would like to say thank you.

Phil Cronin

PART 1
THE EARLY YEARS

At Holy Rosary church in Sunderland, towards the end of the 1950s, the parish priest is debating how best to raise more money from his parishioners. For Father Jeremiah O'Callaghan, the obvious solution lay in a game of bingo. As a game of chance, it appealed to the gambling instincts of his flock and provided them with an excuse for a good night out. It was, he thought, an easy way to bring in the cash. He wasn't quite sure how to go about it but he knew where he might get some help. The stationers in town, Edward Thompson, situated in South Street and Walworth Street, were the local Catholic repository and supplied most of the local Catholic churches. He would ask them. When he walked into the shop, he found himself served by a tall, athletic and personable young man who quickly grasped what was wanted. Grabbing a pad and pencil, Frank Cronin took his first order for bingo tickets. It was an opportunity which would lead to the transformation of the business and Frank Cronin's own career. This small, traditional firm of printers and stationers in Sunderland would become the world's leading supplier of bingo tickets, providing jobs for 1,100 people at its peak. Frank himself would earn the sobriquet 'the king of bingo'.

Edward Thompson was the family business, run at the time by Frank's father, John Louis Cronin, who was the great- nephew of the founder. Edward Thompson had been born in 1843, the son of a carpenter from Birtley near Durham. His father John had moved the family to Sunderland by the early 1850s, attracted by the employment prospects in a rapidly growing town. Situated on the river Wear, Sunderland had long since overtaken Newcastle to become the most important centre for shipbuilding in the region.

The industry was flourishing, supporting a host of other trades alongside it, from marine engineers and anchor, cable and chain makers to boat builders and timber merchants. Thousands of men and women settled in the town, taking its population from 64,000 in 1851 to 125,000 in 1901.

Apprenticed as a stationer, Edward had an entrepreneurial streak and set up his own business in 1867. Gambling, it is said, played an important part in the birth of the new venture for much of the capital apparently came from a winning bet Edward had placed on a horse at Newcastle races. But Edward was surrounded by examples of small entrepreneurs. This was the age of the small businessman and the local trades directory was filled with page after page of them – from basket makers and biscuit makers, cartwrights and clog makers, coopers and cutlers, feather and flock merchants to keepers of livery stables and makers of umbrellas. He opened his business in High Street West, living above the shop with his wife Mary. Very soon he had also taken on his own apprentice, George Curran, the son of his sister Margaret, and added a printing shop. By 1891 Edward and his wife had built their own home, Burn House, on the New Durham Road. After Edward's death in 1898, the business was taken over by George Curran.

It was one of George's sisters, Agnes, who married John Cronin. He was one of the many Irish immigrants who settled in the town during the second half of the nineteenth century. John came to England with his brother from the village of Knocknagree in County Cork. They both worked for Her Majesty's Customs & Excise, with John stationed on the Wear and his brother on the Tyne. John and Agnes had four children: John Louis, the eldest, born in 1896, Winifred, born in 1899, Marguerite, born in 1900, and Donal, born in 1902.

John Louis was a bright boy and attended the Catholic grammar school, St Cuthbert's, in Newcastle, followed by a commercial course at Skerry's College in the city. He completed his studies in 1914, just in time to join up, enlisting in the Artist's Rifles with which he served in France. A big gentle man, well over six feet tall, he had an aptitude for languages and became proficient in French during his military service. He fought on two fronts during the war, serving first in France before completing his service with another regiment in the Middle East. In later life he would enjoy telling his sons how 'me and [General] Allenby conquered Jerusalem' in December 1917.

He came back to Sunderland to join his cousin George Edmonds in the stationery and printing shop. George Curran had died unmarried, leaving the business to his various nephews and nieces. George and John Louis would eventually buy out the interests of their cousins and, after acquiring George's shares, John Louis himself would become the sole owner of the business.

It was not an easy time to begin in business in the north-east. Sunderland's commercial fortunes were tied to shipbuilding and coal which left the town at the whim of world markets. Shipbuilding on the Wear never returned to the level achieved before 1914. In fact, it suffered terribly between the two world wars. By 1926 half of those who had been employed in the industry were out of work. In the town as a whole around a third of the working population was unemployed during the inter-war years. By 1939 only eight shipyards survived of the 16 which had been in operation in 1918. By then Edward Thompson had given up the High Street premises, selling them to Burton, the tailoring chain. John Louis moved the business to 10 South Street, a rabbit-warren of a property, but one which boasted a frontage along Walworth Street as well as South Street. Convinced that shop windows sold a shop, he put in five along the South Street frontage and another six along Walworth Street. This made the shop seem much larger than it was. Although it boasted a separate 'Envelope Department' and 'Card Department', it employed no more than half a dozen people.

It was during these difficult times that Francis Stephen Cronin was born, on 3 February 1933, in a small terraced house in Barnard Street in Sunderland. Always known as Frank, he was John Louis Cronin's second son. The eldest, John Joseph, had been born in 1929, and a third, James Donal Patrick (always known as Jim), was born in 1934. Both John and Jim chose not to follow in their father's footsteps. John would qualify as a chartered accountant, although he eventually returned to the business, while Jim was ordained as a priest in 1959, serving more than 30 years with the African Foreign Mission among the Masai tribesmen of Kenya. Only Frank would choose the family business.

Frank was born with a squint in one eye and until he started school at the age of five he went every week to Dr Margaret Rankin, an ophthalmologist, who gave him eye exercises, using a patch over one eye. By the time he began school, the squint had gone.

It was not long before the family moved from 44 Barnard Street to 27 Westfield Grove, just a few streets away. Frank went to St Joseph's School, Millfield, where he was taught by his father's two sisters, Winnie and Margie. The Irish families settling in Sunderland during the nineteenth century had strengthened the local Catholic community, of which the Cronins were a part, and St Joseph's was one of several new Catholic parishes which had been founded as a result. The Cronins were faithful Catholics, attending mass every week, and there were several priests in both Frank's father's and mother's families. Frank's uncle, Donal Cronin, for example, was a parish priest at St Bede's in Jarrow for many years and was respected for his work among the unemployed during the inter-war depression. Frank's mother had a cousin, Father Joe McNichol, working overseas as a missionary. 'Faith,' recounted Jim Cronin, 'was very important at home.'

Frank's mother, Frances, was a teacher before her marriage. After studying at the Catholic training college at Fenham in Newcastle, she had taught at St Patrick's school in Sunderland. Her father, Stephen Davies, was a Welshman who had served as a crewman on coastal vessels, settling in Sunderland, where he became a steam engine maker and fitter. He and his wife Helen had six daughters, Norah, Annie, Patricia, Frances, Cecilia and Laura. They endured the grief of seeing four of the girls die young, Patricia and Norah at the age of five, Cecilia at 26 and Laura at 18, leaving only Annie and Frances. It is said that all of them died from tuberculosis, a disease rampant throughout Europe until the middle of the twentieth century. It was a terrible and debilitating disease which was brought under control only through the common use of antibiotics after the Second World War. In Britain in 1913, for example, there were 117,000 cases. The usual treatment was rest and fresh air, often at an isolation hospital or sanatorium situated in open countryside. It proved to be of little use – more than half of those entering a sanatorium with the disease were dead within five years.

Sadly Frances herself contracted tuberculosis, first of the lungs and then of the throat, and was often very ill. She spent several spells at the Grampian Sanatorium in Kingussie, near Inverness, opened in 1901 and run after 1934 by the Sisters of Charity of the Order of St Vincent de Paul. Her boys remembered how she was often absent from home for long periods as she recuperated in sanatoria. Frank recalled how 'there were stretches of my life when Mum was not there' and wrote to her often. Jim remembered how she had been away in Scotland for what seemed like months when he was told by his Auntie Annie, a woman he recalled as being as well-built as his mother was slight, that she was coming home at last. He was awoken in the middle of the night as Auntie Annie swept into his bedroom, announcing with a flourish, 'Jim! Here is your Mother!' But Jim, no more than seven or eight years old, in a reaction born of his long separation from her, could only compare her unfavourably with his aunt. 'I looked at her and I looked at Auntie Annie and I was disappointed; there did not seem nearly as much of her as there was of Auntie Annie.' His father would tell him that his mother had been so ill so often that on nine occasions she had been given the last rites. Jim never knew how to respond to enquiries about his mother's health. He remembered she spent most of her time in her dressing gown so he concluded that if she was dressed she must be feeling better. Frank remembered how his father had help in the house from two young women, Nancy Masson and Nancy Carragher. 'I nursed her myself,' Frank recalled. 'I was off school for weeks and weeks to look after my mother.'

By then John, the eldest, was busy with his accountancy examinations, while Jim was away from home, having begun his training for the priesthood when he was 16. Frank's one regret about national service was that it took him away from his mother.

For Jim, despite this sadness, home life was nevertheless ideal, living in an environment of love, wisdom and trust. For Frank, his mother was 'Little Mam', just five feet two inches beside her three tall sons, 'queenly and serene', with immaculate speech and a talent for mimicry. Knowing the value of education, she always encouraged her sons to do well. 'My Mam,' reflected Frank, 'was more spirited than my Dad.' Frances Cronin endured constant suffering until her frailty finally gave way and she died at home at the age of 55 in October 1955. Frank was at home at the time, sitting on the stairs outside the bathroom, conversing with his mother while she was having a bath. He suddenly realised that his mother had stopped talking. There was no response to his shouted queries and knocks on the door, which he had to break down only to find his mother had died. It was a memory which haunted Frank throughout his life to the extent that he would never allow locks on the bathroom doors in his own homes.

The boys' father too had once suffered from tuberculosis, convalescing in the sanatorium at Grindon Hall, converted by the borough council in 1922. He was one of the lucky ones, although Frank remembered how 'he never had a good chest and always walked at a leisurely pace'. Both John Louis and Frances had been ill at the time of their marriage, spending their first days as a married couple living in a hut at Grindon Hall.

Having to look after a very ill wife, three young boys and a business operating in the depths of the depression, even if he did have help in the house, must have taken its toll on John Louis Cronin. Although the family was never poor, money was unpredictable, depending on how well the shop was doing. Most income came in at Christmas time or when the night schools began a new term.

After the depression came another world war. Sunderland, with its shipbuilding yards, became the most heavily bombed English town north of Hull, and the seventh most bombed in the country. The yards were good customers of Edward Thompson, many of them buying stationery from the firm. There were 42 raids on the shipyards, 267 people were killed and more than a thousand injured. More than half the casualties came in two raids which destroyed much of the centre of the town in May 1943. There was an anti-aircraft battery at Tunstall Hill and the sound made by the guns could be heard for miles. Many thought that there was only one gun and this mighty war machine became popularly known locally as 'Big Bertha', after the heavy gun of the First World War. Frank remembered how early in the war one of these guns fired a dud – 'it landed about fourteen14 feet in front of our house and blew all the front windows out'.

Frank recalled an even more dramatic incident during one of the heavy raids on the centre of town. 'I was sleeping with my Dad as a little lad and there was a bloody big bang about three o'clock in the morning. We lived a good two miles from the [printing] factory and there was this huge red glow in the sky.' His father shot out of bed, realising the raid had probably claimed his property. He reached the town centre to discover the door of the premises was open, for his compositor, who lived nearby, was already there. But Edward Thompson had been fortunate – the stick of incendiary bombs, which should have been scattered throughout the building, with devastating effects, was jammed in a split in the heavy main roof beam. The main damage was to the roof. Frank heard from his father, who had been running up and down the yard of the factory, with buckets filled from the single tap, throwing water onto the flames, that 'there was hardly a slate left'.

Frank was still at school. Ray Brown, who later joined Edward Thompson, knew Frank at the time because they were altar servers, together with Frank's other brothers, at the Holy Cross convent of the Little Sisters of the Poor. Frank, recollected Ray, was 'a quiet boy'. But at school Frank developed a taste for singing on stage which allowed him to cast off his self-confessed shyness behind the mask of the performer, boosting his confidence and helping him to overcome his nerves. He would confess that he was 'always a bit of a ham'. His first role was as a king in a short school play. His Auntie Margie encouraged him to take part in school productions of Gilbert & Sullivan and he developed a life-long affection for the music. He often took leading roles, such as the Mikado in the opera of the same name, the Pirate King in *The Pirates of Penzance* and the Grand Inquisitor in *The Gondoliers*. Later he would join three local Gilbert & Sullivan societies, St Benet's, St Joseph's and the Ford and Hilton Lane Operatic Society. On one occasion he was asked by another society to take over the role of the Mikado at short notice. He decided not to attend the dress rehearsal and only turned up on the first night. 'The first thing I had to do was sing a love song to Katisha. There were five girls there but I hadn't a clue which one was Katisha. Which is why I should have gone to the dress rehearsal.' Frank had a gift for remembering music and lyrics and still carries around hundreds of songs in his head. On the scout camps he attended from school, such as the one which took 60 boys from Sunderland to Glenfinnan in Scotland, he was an enthusiastic participant in the shows put on for the locals.

Jim Cronin, younger by just one year, was often at the same camps as his brother for they were both at the same school. When they were young, they had the usual love-hate relationship between siblings with just a year between them. Jim remembered how competitive Frank could be at so young an age, and he himself was often aggressive in fighting his corner as the youngest brother. On one occasion when they were wrestling with each other in the street at Westfield Grove two local boys wandered past, making the mistake of saying 'You Cronins are always fighting'. This was enough to unite the brothers who instantly turned on the two outsiders, roughing them up before resuming their own fight. This was typical of the way Frank would keep an eye out for his younger brother. When the family was still living in Barnard Street, Jim, not yet three years old, slipped under the rear wheel of the milk float as it came past; Frank, just four, hammered on the driver's door to warn him, stopping the float and saving Jim from injury. This mutual support and respect, Jim would later recollect, ran through the family, giving 'that sense of security in the home so you could be yourself'.

Frank was a bright boy and passed his eleven- plus examination, which had just been introduced, allowing him to attend the local Catholic grammar school. Run by the Jesuits, this was known as Corby Hall, changing its name to St Aidan's when it was taken over by the Christian Brothers during Frank's last year. He enjoyed school, discovering he was good at racket sports, and had an aptitude for mathematics. 'Mathematically I was always top of the class. I had a rival but I normally pipped him … I was one of those irritating guys in the class – I got everything right all the time.' Jim Cronin described Frank's mathematical ability at school as 'bordering on genius'. Fascinated by numbers, and the complexities of geometric progressions, for which he was making up his own formulae at the age of 12 or 13, he left other boys behind.

Discipline under the Jesuits was strict and Frank appreciated having the gentle Father Budworth as his form teacher. The Latin master, Father Brennan, on the other hand, Frank detested, particularly because he was always too ready to send boys to be beaten by the prefect of discipline, who could administer up to nine strokes on each hand with the hated ferula. This implement, about twelve inches long, was a piece of flat bone or rubber covered in leather, 'designed', Frank remembered, 'to inflict the maximum amount of pain with the minimum amount of damage'. Frank especially loathed the way Brennan picked on one boy, Gerald Barry. The eldest boy in a large family, who relied on him at home, he would still rise early every morning to act as server for Father Brennan at mass. Yet almost every day Brennan would send Gerald to be beaten for some minor offence, impervious to the boy's circumstances. 'To my mind,' remarked Frank, 'Gerry Barry would end up as a saint in heaven and Brennan would be down burning at the other end. I wouldn't have put up with what Gerry had to put up with, I would have landed one of them.' Brennan was put in his place by Frank's father who had been furious to discover that his son was spending more time writing out lines than on his homework.

Even though Frank sailed through his School Certificate, he did not stay at school. 'Education, entrapped in a school, was very limiting and I always believed that true education started after school.' He was, he says, 'grimly determined' to leave school - he already had a burning desire to join his father in business.

PART 2
THE BUSINESSMAN

1 'LOOKING FOR CHANGE' – FROM STATIONERY TO BINGO TICKETS

In the late 1940s Edward Thompson was still a small jobbing printer's and stationer's, with a host of customers, large and small, from retail customers passing the shop to the large shipyards still active along the river. In the printing shop there was one large old press and a handful of smaller but equally old hand-fed short-run presses. Frank remembered how during the winter months his father would start up the main press in the early hours of the morning to print the stop-press test match scores from Australia on the first editions of the local newspapers. The firm printed everything from large posters to wedding invitations. Many of the local Catholic clergy, who knew there were priests in the Cronin family, came to the firm for their offertory envelopes.

Frank's father was delighted that one of his sons was working alongside him. Frank would later reflect that 'I know my Dad loved me ... he had one son who was a priest, which he thought was great, he had another who was a chartered accountant, which he thought was great, but the one in the middle as far as he was concerned was *the* one, the fact that I wanted to do his job, to go his way, I got to the top of the class in one stride.'. For Frank, his father provided lessons in running a business he never forgot. It had little to do with how to get on in business but everything to do with setting an example in how to treat people. He later recalled how 'my Dad never had more than a dozen people working for him but all of them loved him; he had hundreds of customers but all of them loved him – you couldn't find one with whom he had a wrong word; and every supplier loved him. So where else should I go to learn how to do it than with my Dad?'. Among the long-serving staff was the shop manageress, Bessie New, who kept a close eye on Frank when he started, and the printing foreman, John Connaboy. His father's approach chimed with Frank's already strong belief that the most important of the ten commandments was the fourth, 'Love Thy Neighbour', which he would strive to place at the heart of the business when he eventually took charge. Frank even then appreciated that his father 'didn't have huge ambitions' but he could see that 'he loved life, he loved people, he loved his staff. I thought that was the biggest achievement you could have, to have a happy life'. Throughout his business career one of Frank's strong beliefs was that 'you must never take the human element out of business. The business has to serve the people, not the other way round.'

In the shop Frank soon displayed the persuasive powers which would make him such an outstanding salesman. Before Jim left home to begin his studies for the priesthood, he would often work alongside Frank in the shop. One day a woman came and asked Jim where she could find a card a dog might send its mistress for her birthday. Jim, struck by how lonely someone must be to make such a request, received a sharp kick on the shins from his older brother, their signal that Frank would take over the sale. Persuading the customer that the shop had plenty of choice in suitable cards, he added that it was better to buy three cards rather than one. The customer agreed and left the shop feeling her needs had been met while Frank had secured a good sale.

Frank's training was interrupted in 1951 when he began his national service. Between 1945 until 1963 two and a half million young men were called up at the rate of 6,000 every week for national service. The two years spent in the armed forces was a mixed experience for some young men but Frank had no regrets about his time in the Royal Air Force. 'There was a tremendous camaraderie among the potpourri thrown together by complete accident.' He formed long-lasting friendships with the two young men, Ken Bumfrey and Bill Meikle, whom he found sleeping on either side of him at their first billet in Padgate. In 1939 a small RAF station was built just outside this small village near Warrington in Lancashire which provided basic training for wartime recruits. During national service many thousands of young men like Frank Cronin were first admitted into the RAF through the gates of RAF Padgate. It was in the RAF that Frank first began playing squash, which would become a lifelong addiction. Friends were expected to stick together in this strange new world and help each other out – Frank, who never touched alcohol, even in his youth, remembered being told off by an irate Bill Meikle for failing to prevent him drinking too much and ruining his suit as a result.

Most RAF recruits spent just a week at Padgate before being sent elsewhere to do most of their square-bashing but Frank stayed longer. He eventually left for a posting to the RAF wireless school at Yatesbury, near Calne in Wiltshire. Opened during the First World War, Yatesbury was one of the RAF's oldest airfields, becoming a radar and radio school during the 1930s, which it remained until it was closed in 1969. Frank spent 16 months training as an air wireless mechanic, rising, he remembered, 'to the dizzy heights of a senior aircraftsman but I did do original design work in the RAF as a junior'. He found the work fascinating, discovering an outlet for his ability to think laterally and his talent for problem solving. This was not always appreciated. Frank devised a method of cleaning electric brushes mechanically rather than by hand which gave him time for an extra cup of coffee – but left his sergeant with the challenge of finding more work for him to do. (Frank experienced, like many others, some of the pointlessness of the tasks set for national servicemen. When a senior officer was due to make an inspection, their sergeant, eager to make sure that his men were all occupied, gave them buckets filled with nuts and bolts to sort out; Frank had to repeat the process for finishing too early.)

Frank applied the knowledge he gained from his training when he returned to Sunderland, setting up Wearside Electronics a few years later. 'I always had it in mind because I was determined to use my skills.' By the time he finished his national service, his father was in his early fifties and the business little changed – 'He was', recalled

Frank, 'happy and content, drifting into retirement'. Frank, on the other hand, in his early twenties, intelligent and energetic, was looking for ways the business could grow. There were inevitable tensions between father and son. There had been little investment in the printing shops for years yet when Frank wanted to replace an old Heidelberg platen press, his father resisted. Set in his ways, he failed to understand why a machine which had worked so well for so long needed to go. As Frank recollected, 'I was more looking for change than he was, I was more looking for progress, for doing it better'. While his father had been content to wait for the business to come to him, Frank went out in search of business. He visited existing customers, like the shipyards, winning bigger orders. For instance, the shop made only an occasional sale of tracing paper to the yards, which needed supplies for their draughtsmen, but through calling on the yards Frank was able to persuade them to take larger quantities. Frank also sought out new customers, travelling down the coast to resorts like Whitby, Scarborough and Bridlington, selling novelties. He had an eye for an opportunity. He would pass the buyer for Blacketts, the local department store, every morning on his way to the bus stop. He made a point of getting to know him and eventually won a major order. Bigger orders produced bigger discounts from suppliers which allowed the firm to pass on lower prices and attract more customers.

Frank's passion for selling was given further encouragement when the business had to move to smaller premises with even less space for displays. After the war the shop was almost like an island surrounded by a sea of destruction in the centre of Sunderland. The borough council finally decided to redevelop the area in the late 1950s but as the firm received minimal compensation it was compelled to find a smaller property over three floors, opposite the Empire Theatre and next to the Palace Cinema. Later the shop would move again, this time to Fawcett Street, opposite Woolworths, which created much more passing business.

Frank's drive was noticed by one young apprentice who later became his right-hand man. Tom Clark was still at school when he became a part-time errand boy at Edward Thompson in 1953, delivering parcels on the bus to local Catholic churches. After leaving school in 1956, he would take up a permanent job at the firm as an apprentice printer, by which time Frank had become managing director. Frank, remembered Tom, developed a numbering and dating system for overprinting offertory envelopes, a precursor of the system he would devise for printing bingo tickets. The year after taking over the business, Frank became a married man. He had met Teresa Martin shortly after the death of his mother. With Frank the only son left at home, his father came to rely upon him more and more. When he asked for his usual cup of tea one afternoon, Frank discovered there was no milk left. Taking one of his mother's dainty jugs, he walked down Westfield Grove to the house of some family friends, the Macdonalds. He knocked and waited on the doorstep. 'The door opened and there was this dream of a girl, she was absolutely gorgeous.' She was rather brusque with the tall young man carrying a fancy milk jug. A little later, Mrs Macdonald, whom Frank knew as Aunty Bridgie, rang him up. When she had discovered he had the car, she asked him to run Theresa home. 'That', Frank would recall, 'helped to make the job easy!' Aunty Bridgie proved a valuable ally, putting in a good word for him when her cousin, Teresa's mother, Callie Martin, asked after this young man who was courting her daughter. Teresa's father, Jack, was a master butcher with his own shop in Ryhope and often greeted Frank with the words, 'That bloody long fellow's here again!' His daughter was the youngest of three children, with two brothers, Jim, who became a mining engineer, and Tom, a teacher. Teresa worked in the dispensary in the local Co-op in Hetton- le-Hole. Frank had known about her a long time. 'She'd always been one of the girls that I had been aware of at school – this girl was very pretty, very nice.' After three dates they knew they were made for each other and she accepted his proposal without hesitation. 'It was pretty quick ... we had been taught as Catholics that you don't mess a girl around, that you state your intentions ... she said yes immediately, neither of us played games with each other ... we were both besotted with each other.' Apparently Teresa had to make up her mind quickly. The story goes that Frank proposed to her as they were crossing the river by ferry. When she asked for time to think about it, he told her she had 15 minutes before they reached the other side. The couple were engaged for over a year before they were married, on 15 July 1957, at St Michael's, Houghton-le-Spring, followed by a honeymoon in the Lake District. The marriage would last for nearly 50 years, broken only by Teresa's death in January 2004. She became the bedrock of Frank's life as he began concentrating on building the family business.

2 'PICKING CHERRIES OFF A TREE' — THE BINGO BOOM

When the six feet seven inch frame of Father Jeremiah O'Callaghan loomed above the counter in the South Street shop one day in the late 1950s, no one had any idea that his request would be the catalyst for utterly changing the business. He asked John Louis if he could supply him with bingo tickets for the next parish fund-raiser. 'No problem at all, Jerry. I'll sort that out for you,' responded John Louis as the priest left the shop, immediately turning to Frank and saying, 'You can do that, Frank'.

Frank made investigations and discovered that W S Cowell Ltd of Ipswich printed the Bernard series of bingo tickets. 'So I bought them, and you could buy them in eight different colours, and 1,800 combinations, and that was it.' When the tickets arrived, Frank laboriously pinned them all into separate books. Cowell's had begun printing bingo tickets at the beginning of the Second World War. The Royal Navy believed that bingo was the ideal game for keeping naval ratings relaxed yet alert while they were at sea. They wanted tickets to supply the Mediterranean fleet but paper was even scarcer in Malta, the fleet's base, than in the UK. The Navy asked for help from the Malta branch of the naval outfitters, Bernard's of Harwich. Bernard's acquired the copyright to the combinations which were in use and had the tickets printed by Cowell's, which had previously done work for Bernard's.

Father O'Callaghan will have known just how successful bingo sessions were in raising funds for the church. The Catholic Church had never held the extreme views about gambling taken by other churches and had made the most of the minor changes in the law which had made it possible for quasi-commercial games of bingo to be held, providing the profits all went to charity. So widespread was the use of bingo for fund-raising throughout the Catholic Church that many participants were convinced the game had been invented by the Church.

Of course, the origins of the game went back much further. Something similar was being played by working women in London in the early eighteenth century when the first state lottery was also organised. Illegal, private lotteries were also popular, particularly with women, who would pay as little as a halfpenny for a ticket. The game was taken up by the Royal Navy in Malta in the early nineteenth century and eventually given official approval under the name of 'tombola'. The British army had adopted 'house' by the beginning of the twentieth century. The elements of the game were well-established, using the numbers 1 – 90, with five figures in each row, marked off as the numbers were called out from balls drawn from a bag. Frank's father told him how he had played bingo in the trenches. Many servicemen brought the game back with them, introducing it to servicemen's and working men's clubs. Although commercial gambling was effectively outlawed, the game was illicitly played up and down the country and was particularly popular at fairgrounds and seaside resorts. During the inter-war years the name 'bingo' began to be applied to the game. The claim that the name originated in the USA is disputed, with evidence suggesting it was already in use in England around the same time. It was only in the 1950s that the new name overtook the use of 'tombola' or 'housey-housey'. Even when Frank Cronin established a separate company to handle the bingo business, he combined the two more traditional names for the game by calling it Tombola House Ltd.

Father O'Callaghan was certainly pleased with the service Frank gave him. As the word spread, other priests and parishes began placing orders for tickets. The firm also began supplying working men's clubs, which were particularly strong in the north-east, with 30 or more in Sunderland alone. All this quickly made the original Sunderland premises too small. In 1959 Frank moved the printing operation to an old flour mill in Wilson Street North, in the area known as Sheepfolds on the northern side of the river. The mill was bought for pennies, remembered Frank,; it was 'cheap space'. He could use the basement for the heavy printing machinery and the three upper floors for lighter equipment. Having more storage space was equally important not only for the increasing volume of paper the printing presses were consuming, but also because there had to be a separate picking point for every customer. 'Initially you take what you can manage with the coppers you've got. I didn't pay very much for it ... It was a foot-in-the-water exercise – you don't dive in until you know what the temperature is.' He never believed in leasing or renting assets – when one supplier later offered to provide an orange-juice machine for the staff canteen provided Frank bought the orange juice from him, Frank refused because he wanted to own the machine – and always avoided borrowing money. Ray Brown, who joined the company in 1963, remembered that 'Frank was always a very careful person, he would not go into debt for anything'.

Edward Thompson's success with local churches and working men's clubs showed that there was obvious potential for bingo on a commercial scale. Loopholes in the law already made it quite easy to establish regular bingo sessions in many parts of the country. Mass games were common in the holiday camps which sprang up after the war, raising many thousands of pounds for charity. Reforms intended to regulate gambling actually opened the floodgates to commercial bingo. The Betting and Gaming Act, 1960, not only made it legitimate to establish bingo clubs provided stake money was returned to the players, but also made it possible to make a charge for the right to take part in a game.

The legislation came into effect on 1 January 1961 and the first commercial bingo club opened two days later. There were long waiting lists to join the new clubs and the first games attracted long queues of eager players. Within two years commercial bingo clubs had more than 14 million members. The game was criticised for attracting many older women on limited incomes, posing the danger that bingo threatened to turn them into gambling addicts, throwing away money they could ill-afford to lose. Even today women still make up three-quarters of bingo players. But Frank Cronin believed that bingo revolutionised the social lives of many women in the north-east. In a society dominated by male culture to an extent many would find difficult to comprehend half a century later, bingo clubs gave many working-class women a largely female social focus where it was possible for them to gather on their own during the day or in the evenings. As one newspaper put it, 'A housewife's bingo stake is the equivalent of her husband's beer, baccy and betting money'. Frank would later tell a journalist that 'those halls are important. When they began in 1961, they were in their way a major part of the women's liberation movement in this country. They were a place where a lady could go for an evening, entirely on her own at a time when she could not go into a pub alone. She could meet friends, eat a snack and feel entirely at home. It was a revolution, especially in the north'. Recent research has confirmed that bingo clubs have made an important contribution to the social lives of many women.

The boom transformed Edward Thompson. The company's growth was phenomenal. Turnover doubled every year for several years. From less than a dozen employees in 1959, the company was employing more than 300 just six years later. From selling a few thousand tickets supplied by someone else every month, the company was printing 50 million each week by 1965. Thanks to his dexterity with numbers, Frank Cronin expanded the number of combinations for use with bingo tickets from less than 2,000 to nearly 17,000, keeping pace with the incessant growth in the size of games run by the expanding commercial operators. The company branched out into sales of bingo equipment as well as bingo tickets and supplied customers at home and overseas. Edward Thompson printed the tickets, Tombola House handled the collation, binding and distribution of the books of tickets, and Wearside Electronics developed bingo equipment. New factories were built for Wearside Electronics in Wilson Street North and for Edward Thompson in nearby Richmond Street.

How did Frank Cronin achieve such success for Edward Thompson? Firstly, the company was in an advantageous position as bingo boomed. The firm drew on its earlier experience in selling bingo tickets to local churches and working men's clubs. It was driven by Frank's outstanding mathematical talent and his entrepreneurial spirit, determined to make the most of every opportunity which came along. Knowing little about the game, many newcomers to the industry turned to Frank Cronin, still just 27 when the boom began, for help and advice. Frank was happy to advise them. 'You had to think about the mathematics from the start because the trouble was that your customers weren't mathematicians so you guided them through the whole thing, really. I would have to tell them how to do it.' Word spread about his knowledge and fantastic mathematical ability. People in the industry would come to him with ideas for games and he always helped them to work out the details. Edward Thompson gained the reputation for being 'the bingo people', to the extent that gaming inspectors even spent part of their training at the company.

One of the firm's earliest commercial bingo customers was a local cinema chain and in the long-term the most successful commercial bingo operators would emerge from the national cinema chains. Cinema-going had been in decline since the end of the Second World War. Although the number of people visiting a British cinema reached a record of more than 31 million weekly admissions in 1946, this figure fell to 21 million in 1956 and 10 million in 1960. The decline would continue until the mid-1980s. It was a sign of social change – as prosperity returned, more people could afford to rent or buy their own televisions while the advent of a teenage culture brought alternative recreation for young people, previously one of the staple cinema-going groups. But cinema chains were faced with the problem of what to do with the huge picture palaces which had been built during the heyday of film. Some were demolished, others were turned into dance halls, concert halls and bowling alleys, but none of these alternative uses lasted long. For the cinema operators, bingo proved a lifeline; for others, it proved an opportunity.

Initially cinema operators devised what was called cine-bingo. Recently, this term has been revived to describe bingo played in front of a cinema screen, with a live caller linking several games. The cine-bingo devised in the early 1960s was designed to attract more customers through cinema doors by putting on a bingo session between programmes. As one cine-bingo operator told

Frank, he had to give his customers what they were asking for.

But Frank Cronin believes that the move away from cine-bingo, abandoning films altogether in favour of converting cinemas into bingo clubs, began not with the national chains but with fairground operators. Among them was local showman Max Testo who had been running bingo games at fairs for years (he would later call his chain of bingo halls, 'Fair World'). With cine-bingo taking away business from fairground bingo, Max became one of the first to take a redundant cinema and turn it into a bingo club; he was also one of the first customers to ask Frank for larger combinations. 'The thing about Max was that if you gave him something that worked, he would come along for something that worked better, and something that worked better again, and he pushed the boat out, and the big cinema chains followed him, rather than the other way round. The big show people were more into bingo than the cinemas were.' Another showman was Bill Noble who founded the Noble Organisation.

Many of the cinemas supplied by Edward Thompson on the cine-bingo circuit would become bingo clubs. All the national cinema chains turned to bingo, from Rank and ABC to Granada and Essoldo. Rank started turning cinemas into bingo halls from 1961, transforming many local Odeons and Gaumonts into Top Rank Social Clubs, while the first ABC conversion in Walthamstow retained the ABC name as the Alpha Bingo Club. Where the cinema chains had ventured, the dance halls followed, for they too were fighting declining popularity. The most significant example was Mecca Dance Halls. Under Eric Morley, who also introduced bingo based on 75 numbers to the UK from the United States, Mecca not only converted existing dance halls but also bought up old cinemas for conversion into bingo clubs. Mecca's rapid progress highlights the astonishing growth of the game – by February 1961, one month after the new legislation came into effect, Mecca was already using 50,000 books of bingo tickets every week. By June it was selling half a million every week, with an average of 150,000 players every day. They were attracted by free publicity in the press, celebrity callers, from Diana Dors and Cilla Black to Max Bygraves and Tommy Steele, and prizes which as well as cash featured exotic foreign holidays, jewellery and even dishwashers, an almost unheard-of luxury at the time. The National Golden Scoop Club, linking several hundred clubs together, was able to offer cash prizes exceeding £4,000, worth in excess of £100,000 today, based on the change in average earnings.

Such linked games – which strictly-speaking were illegal – used the larger combinations devised by Frank Cronin. These were a critical factor in the company's success. With much more valuable prizes at stake, and hundreds of participants, larger combinations reduced the risk of fraud and the likelihood of multiple winners (bingo players hated the idea of sharing their winnings and the idea that one player could win the jackpot was one of the main attractions of bingo). Frank had begun devising his own combinations when his original supplier failed to meet Edward Thompson's request for more tickets in response to demand. When he was told he could not have the supplies he needed to meet his orders, Frank decided he would have to replicate the tickets himself. 'They told us at one point that they could only let us have 3,000 a month, although we were selling 10,000 a month with ease. We thought about it and decided to print our own cards.' Since Frank did not own the copyright, this got him into trouble, despite the fact, as he strongly pointed out, that the supplier had failed to fulfil his order. He had to pay compensation for copyright infringement although his negotiating skills ensured that 'they did not get the money they were looking for'.

'Bingo was getting into its stride and before long the printing of bingo cards was our main concern,' Frank would later tell the local newspaper. The challenge of producing ever larger combinations appealed to Frank's mathematical brain. He knew that, given every game used a pool of 90 numbers, with every ticket featuring a selection of 15, there were in theory more than 45 thousand million million different combinations (45, 795, 673, 964, 460, 816, to be exact). Frank seized the chance to devise his own combinations – 'What I liked to do', he would say, 'was to move faster than the other guys ... normally they were chasing me rather than ahead of me.'

He began with 3,000 and would eventually reach 16,800. This, he remembered, 'put the competition in real trouble'. From the outset he made sure he owned the copyright of the new combinations. One unique characteristics was that every ticket differed from the next by five numbers, which, Frank had calculated, was the mathematical optimum. The tickets of most rivals differed by only two numbers per ticket. For commercial bingo operators, Frank's system proved very attractive, with its larger combinations and numbering scheme, guaranteeing a single winner in 90 per cent of games. It gave Edward Thompson a clear advantage over its rivals and would turn the company into one of the largest of its kind in the world. Even today, Frank says, 'There is no other combination in the world which works as well as ours'. According to Ray Brown, 'The Edward Thompson combination was generally recognised as being the best you could get'. This helped the company to claim Rank, the cinema chain, and Mecca, the dance hall group, as major customers as they became two of the leading bingo club operators in the country. They chose Edward Thompson precisely because other suppliers could not match Frank's larger combinations which made big bingo sessions possible.

Frank's facility with numbers was awesome. Often he would calculate answers in his head or simply make a few calculations on a scrap of paper. His skill was shown when Frank's combinations came under closer scrutiny. As the bingo club chains grew in size, the clubs were ever more anxious to prevent the nightmare of hundreds of winners. In the late 1960s Frank was asked to devise a completely new game for Top Rank, the bingo offshoot of the Rank Organisation. One day he received a call from Top Rank's managing director who told him that a professor of maths had been asked to analyse the game and had concluded it would indeed yield hundreds of winners. Asked to visit Top Rank's headquarters in

London, Frank took the train from Sunderland the following morning and, on reaching the office, was left alone for an hour with the pile of computer listing paper containing the complex mathematical analysis made by the professor. When the managing director came to see him, Frank told him that he had marked up the errors in the professor's analysis. Although he was impressed with the professor's work, he was convinced that the game was sound and committed himself to underwriting the risk of having more than one winner. Frank, of course, was right. As he later said, 'The motivation for making sure a game works is because it is your livelihood, not an academic exercise'.

In the early days producing combinations was laborious and time-consuming. Linda Holden joined the firm from school in 1966. She remembered Frank interviewed her while he sat with his feet on the desk. She began on the switchboard in the office above Wearside Electronics before moving to accounts. For a time she was also part of the team of young women working on combinations. Each line on every ticket had to be checked manually against all other previous lines, the details of which were entered in green ledgers. Tom Clark recalled how counters were used to work out new combinations. It would take a full day to compile six bingo tickets with new combinations of numbers. When the Richmond Street factory was completed in 1965, it included a 'Computations Room' containing files of 250,000 bingo cards stretching back four years, covering every combination printed by the firm.

Edward Thompson occupied an almost unchallenged position in the industry for many years but it was not without rivals. The company met the competition and retained and expanded its customer base by its emphasis on service. One of Frank's maxims was never to say no to a customer – he always took the order first and only then began thinking how it could be met. This was his instinct from the very moment he joined the business and the bingo boom simply reaffirmed it. In London, for instance, the company won a lot of business because it offered delivery in days rather than the six or seven weeks quoted by rivals. 'It was so easy,' remembered Brian Walsh, who joined the company as a salesman in London in 1966, 'it was like picking cherries off a tree.'

One of the reasons all this worked was because of the able lieutenants and hard-working employees Frank recruited. Frank was always in control of the business, making every important decision, but he soon realised he could not run the ever-growing business single-handed. Over the years he gathered together a committed group of managers. Alan Crawford was probably the first when he was invited to become Frank's partner in Tombola House. His family bookbinding firm, Mawson's, based in Villiers Street in Sunderland, had worked for Edward Thompson for a long time, and Frank valued his expertise. Eventually Alan Crawford sold his stake back to Frank and returned to the family business.

Three other managers from the early years of the bingo boom were Jim Hennessy, Tony Strutt and Ernie Dawson. 'Jim Hennessy', said Frank, 'would have walked through fire for me'. He had been working at Pemberton's paper mill when Frank recruited him to manage the bingo section, where he became works manager. Born and bred in Gateshead, he was a tough man who had served in the Royal Navy during the war but he was very fair and earned the respect of the staff. Although he could be dour, he was, said Frank, 'autocratic in a genial sort of way ... that requires a tremendous amount of skill'. For a number of younger men working their way up through the business, Hennessy was an influential mentor. Frank contrasted him with Tony Strutt. Coming from the family which helped to found Strutt & Parker, Strutt was the great-grandson of the second Lord Rayleigh. With his cut-glass accent and aristocratic origins, he could scarcely have been more of a contrast to Hennessy. Twenty years older than Frank, Strutt had flown with the RAF during the war, become a test pilot, and attained the rank of group captain. Ray Brown recalled that he was a man of many parts. He had suffered a broken jaw from a biplane accident in Iraq during the 1930s, taken part in the 1936 Winter Olympics and designed a flight simulator. Like Ray Brown, Strutt also came from Pyrex, and directly approached Frank when Wearside Electronics was being

John Louis Cronin (seated) with his younger brother Donal.

The young Frank.

The schoolboy - Frank is third from the left in the back row

The Cronin family -
(back) Frank, Jim
and John, with
John Louis and
Frances Cronin.

The national
serviceman -
Frank in the RAF.

The extended family - (back) John, Rita, Ronnie, Frank, Maureen, Frances's sister; (front) John Louis, his sisters Margie and Winnie, and Frances. Rita, Ronnie and Maureen were Frank's cousins. Jim was taking the picture.

Frank and Teresa on their wedding day.

John Louis Cronin in later life.

The young entrepreneur. The map shows all the bingo clubs Frank supplied in the UK.

A typical 1960s bingo club in a converted cinema.

The Wilson Street factory with Frank's Jaguar parked outside.

An overseas visits, possibly to Italy, in the late 1960s - (left to right) Frank, Tom Clark, Jim Hennessy, John Louis, unknown.

Frank and his team at a trade show.
The outfits worn by the Edward Thompson girls were designed by Frank

Frank 'doing the cheques' in his Richmond Street office.

An Edward Thompson
brochure from the 1970s.

all together we print

edward thompson group
with an express national free delivery service by our own transport

Frank with his directors and their wives (left to right) Val Clark, Mary Smith, Teresa, Frank, unknown, Tom Clark and Ray Smith.

Frank in New York. He travelled all over the world on business.

The squash player.

Frank and Teresa made a handsome couple.

The growing family - Teresa at home in Appleforth Avenue with Stephen, Paul and Philip (in the pram).

Christmas in the Cronin household at 60 Whitburn Road.

Teresa and her boys.

Frank visiting Jim in Kenya in the 1970s.

Frank was awarded the Silver Heart for his Variety Club work in 1976.

This picture of Frank was taken at Roker Park, Sunderland Football Club's old ground.

The successful family in 1982 - Frank, Teresa and the boys.

developed. His experience in electronics made him an ideal appointment and he helped to design the first bingo equipment, including blower machines and scoreboards. He stayed with the business for several years and made a valuable contribution. Ernie Dawson had been in the same class as Frank at school. Frank appointed him in 1966 as the firm was growing rapidly to help him handle sales and marketing.

Frank recruited several young men who later became instrumental in helping to run the business. Tom Clark, Ray Brown, Ray Smith and Brian Walsh would all become directors. Looking back on the people he assembled, Frank concluded that 'we had a fabulous team'.

Frank gained great satisfaction from making jobs available for local people. The number grew steadily, climbing from 300 in 1965 to 500 five years later. At a time when the town's traditional employers were in decline – headlines in the local newspaper spoke of battles to save jobs at yards like Swan Hunter and the closure of others, such as the Palmers' Yard – Frank was conscious that the job opportunities offered by Edward Thompson were a precious commodity. He knew many households depended on the wages of each of the people he employed. They often worked day and night shifts, supplemented by casual staff employed during holidays. It was commonly believed that you had to be a Catholic to work at Edward Thompson but this story developed only because Frank often employed young men and women who were leaving St Anthony's, one of the local Catholic schools. Frank's father, John Louis, who had grown up during a period when Catholics were still fighting for acceptance in British society, firmly believed that every single employee was Catholic and Frank was content for him to do so.

Frank believed in looking after his staff. When a new factory was built in Richmond Street, Frank made sure it was equipped with a canteen, surgery, sick bay and nurse. Vending machines provides drinks during breaks and employees worked to music piped from records played on a radiogram in an upstairs office. Frank knew everyone's first name and insisted on being called by his first name. He knew something about each employee and their families. Linda Holden recalled how this young dynamic businessman 'gave you confidence in yourself, he looked after you, you felt part of a team'. There were annual outings and an annual staff dance, held originally at the Mecca Ballroom in Sunderland. He would help out staff who were in trouble and encouraged them to come to him if they had any problems. He was a strong believer in training and encouraged staff to take day-release courses to improve their qualifications. A bonus scheme gave workers the chance to increase their earnings. The first one paid by Frank was worth three times average wages. Until the 1980s, Frank recalled, bonuses were 'always fantastic' and a great incentive – 'the work got done all the time'.

The mill in Wilson Street North was only ever a short-term solution. Spread over four storeys, with wooden staircases and squeaky floors, it was never a practical proposition. While the printing works was ideally located in the basement, any waste paper had to be hauled up to the fourth floor for baling before being sent down again. The first new building was the factory to house Wearside Electronics, erected next door to the mill in 1963. Frank had the foresight to realise that the business would need even more space and he soon began acquiring more property around the mill, mainly in Richmond Street. The company's healthy cashflow – and the impressive margins the business enjoyed from its commanding position during the early days of commercial bingo – made it possible to buy every property he wanted. Brian Walsh remembered that the company was awash with cash. Visiting Sunderland to collect reimbursement for his expenses, the accountant, Alec Oliver, paid him from wads of notes in his back pocket – 'it was phenomenal'. The business, remembered Madge Johnson, who joined the company in 1967, 'was printing money' in the 1960s.

Work began on a second purpose-built factory in Richmond Street in 1964. Completed a year later at a cost of £25,000, it contained offices, a despatch department and printing and composing rooms, housing 13 Heidelberg presses consuming 50 tons of paper each week.

This was all the result of what seemed to be the unstoppable growth in bingo. As one newspaper put it at the time, 'The big bingo bubble shows no signs of bursting'. It had, continued the paper, become 'part of the British way of life, like football, cricket and working men's clubs'. Twenty million visits were being made each week to bingo clubs across the country, compared with just five and a half million cinema visits. During 1967-68 the number of commercial bingo clubs increased from 1,634 to 2,254. In one week alone, three new clubs opened in Newcastle, including a city-centre club with a capacity for 1,800 players which enrolled 19,000 members before opening day. This was not unusual. Another club of a similar size opened in Scunthorpe with 6,000 paid-up members. Taking into account working men's clubs, village and church halls, kiosks and fairgrounds, it was reckoned that the actual number of groups regularly playing bingo was over 20,000.

Given this enormous growth, it was hardly surprising that, as Frank Cronin put it, 'it was hands on everywhere' at Edward Thompson. When Ray Brown joined the company, he worked evenings even while he was serving his notice at his previous employer – 'they were just so busy'. To cope with orders, Frank organised a twilight shift from six until nine in the evening for young girls and older women. Once an order had been completed – and the girls in the factory would often work from eight in the morning until ten in the evening, six or seven days a week, alongside the twilight shift, to meet deadlines – the completed books of tickets were loaded into the company's growing fleet of vans for distribution all over the UK. Even the cavernous Standard Vanguard estate belonging to maintenance manager John Hare was pressed into service at peak times. By the end of the 1960s there were 60 vans delivering tickets as well as a UK sales force of 15 and a service depot with five staff in Dublin. Madge Johnson recalled night shifts had to be introduced in the office in order to process the huge number of invoices. In his office, Frank Cronin had a wall map of the UK covered in pins marking the location of clubs served by the company. Customers ranged from local clubs to national chains. The most important was Top Rank, the bingo offshoot of the Rank Organisation, which was buying 85 per cent of its bingo tickets from Edward Thompson by the late 1960s.

Frank Cronin often travelled down to London to meet Top Rank's chief buyer, Alex Slatter, but he disliked staying in hotels. Brian Walsh was tasked with making any bookings. One of Frank's foibles was an insistence that All Bran should be available at breakfast. There would be hell to pay if it wasn't, and Brian often had to buy a box from the nearest shop. Eventually Frank would take to travelling with a box in his suitcase. Frank also hated air-conditioning systems and resented hotels where he was unable to open the window. Instead of hotels, Frank liked to stay in Tottenham, at the home of Len Jenkins, the manager of the Star bingo club in Bruce Grove, and his wife Doris. Brian was courting their daughter Beth at the time but was just completing his long convalescence after a kidney infection, and was at a loose end. Frank heard all about this from Len and one morning threw his car keys at Brian and told him he would be driving Frank to meet with Cowell's in Ipswich. It was after that journey that he offered Brian a job, wanting to cut down his own sales trips to London. Three months later, after training in Sunderland, Brian took over responsibility for selling bingo tickets in London. He was paid £10 a week, with £5 guaranteed, and earned commission of 2.5 per cent on all sales over £200 – 'I earned a fortune in those days'. His area quickly expanded beyond London to cover the south coast with its seaside resorts, and extended north to Cambridge and west to Wales. 'There was not a single bingo club I did not visit.'

Frank continued to come down to London to visit Alex Slatter and Brian remembered how they often ended up in Soho at Raymond's Revue Bar with its scantily clad girls. When one of them came over to take orders for drinks, Frank, a teetotaller, asked for a glass of milk. The girl replied politely that they did not serve milk but Alex Slatter beckoned her over. He whispered to her that if she found a glass of milk, record sales of whisky would follow, for Frank was just lining his stomach in anticipation of the rest of the night. Frank got his milk.

On his trips to London Frank liked to be given a challenge. On one occasion Brian Walsh asked him to see if he could sign up the small chain of Dara bingo clubs, which he had been wooing in vain for several months. Within 24 hours Frank had set up an appointment with the managing director, Brian Tressider. Frank rarely used bad language but when he came back from the meeting he swore at Brian. He told him he could not have picked a more difficult person to sell to – Tressider turned out to be the London agent for Bernard's bingo tickets. But in a testament to Frank's persuasive powers, Tressider had given Brian Walsh a trial order within the week which eventually led to Edward Thompson supplying all seven clubs in the chain.

The scale on which bingo was played alarmed politicians and by the late 1960s there were veiled threats from the government that new legislation would bring an end to commercial bingo. The 1968 Gaming Act did impose strong regulations over an industry which had previously been largely unregulated but the major bingo club chains, thanks to the opposition organised by Eric Morley of Mecca and the widespread popularity of the game, emerged largely unscathed. The new law reinforced the dominance of the national chains as many independent clubs closed because they could not meet the stringent new regulations. There was also consolidation among the chains. In 1970 the Star Group, the largest of the chains, with 114 clubs and two and a half million members, took over the clubs operated by ABC, while in 1973 Ladbroke acquired the Essoldo clubs, renaming them Lucky Seven Bingo. Edward Thompson continued to expand. In 1970 two more floors were added to the Richmond Street factory, when a large art department was also established. By then, the company was the largest manufacturer of bingo tickets in the world, turning out one hundred million every week. It was, remembered Ray Smith, a business 'on the move' under a 'dynamic and very aggressive' Frank Cronin.

Edward Thompson did not just sell bingo tickets. Frank had seen the potential in supplying all the equipment and accessories needed by bingo clubs. This too was driven by customer demand. From an early date the company had printed club membership cards, and, under Tony Strutt, Wearside Electronics developed equipment for many different aspects of the game, including blower machines (the traditional method of calling by drawing numbers from a bag had been replaced by the blower which selected numbers from plastic balls in glass cabinets) and scoreboards. As prizes increased in value, more secure alternative methods were sought to the original blowers which were unsophisticated and easy to manipulate. Through Wearside Electronics, Edward Thompson later introduced a new bingo random selector, described as 'the first major automatic computerised Bingo unit which involved a patented selection process and gave a security system which would meet the most stringent demands'. Many of these ideas came from Frank. He believed innovation came from solving problems rather than an isolated spark of genius: 'The problem came and then I would scratch my head and then you would bring in the engineers ... and eventually you'd get a solution'. One example was the ball-varnishing machine Frank dreamed up. The numbers on the surface of the plastic bingo balls were printed in black ink but they tended to fade after the balls had been jostled together in the blowers time after time. To make the numbers, and thus the balls, last longer, Frank came up with the idea of coating the balls in varnish, a simple and very cost-effective solution.

The constant improvement made by clubs to the facilities they offered brought even greater opportunities. With so many people wanting to play the game, the clubs, noted one press article, very soon 'exploited it with lusher surroundings, bigger prize money, cosier club amenities: everything to keep the clients, mostly middle-aged women, content'. The licensing authorities would consider applications to serve alcohol only if the clubs indicated that they would be moving away from the traditional cinema seating by installing tables and chairs which gave players more space. Brian Walsh found a firm based in Derbyshire which was already supplying clubs with a fixed unit of a table and four seats. The company also began quoting for the conversion work involved in the modernisation of clubs, such as levelling the raked flooring. This led Brian to move to Sunderland to concentrate on selling everything other than bingo tickets, from office equipment and electronic bingo machines to public address systems and background music machines. This venture proved so successful – and won customers beyond bingo, such as supermarkets - that it would lead to the formation in 1975 of a contracts division within the company under Brian Walsh's direction. By the early 1970s, it was said of the company that 'so wide has the diversification been on the bingo side since the first bingo tickets were printed that the company could now take an empty building and furnish it as a bingo hall'.

With such a strong presence in the UK market, it was not long before Frank Cronin began looking overseas for business. From the earliest days of commercial bingo the company had been receiving a steady trickle of enquiries from all over the world. They were infrequent and any orders were usually small but Frank believed that any sale was a foot in the door of another country. Once you gained a toehold, experience would teach him, it almost always brought repeat business. He believes that the first time he travelled overseas was to France although the first orders came from Australasia and North America. It was business which expanded only gradually. As Frank recounted, 'If you were a lad from Sunderland, going down to the big city, going down to London was overseas.'

One of the most important avenues for developing exports was the international exhibition circuit. The company regularly exhibited at what is now the Amusement Trades Exhibition International (ATEI) event, held every year in London, and Frank attended similar exhibitions around the world, from Rome and Paris, Melbourne and Sydney to Chicago and Los Angeles. For Frank these were hugely important. In non-English-speaking countries they helped him with languages. They allowed him to meet his customers and heard what they thought about the company. He could see the latest technological developments and keep an eye on his rivals. Taking staff along helped them to understand that the company was looking ahead. And they were a source of new orders. Advertising, he believed, was much less effective. Selling itself not on price but on service, Edward Thompson one year had no hesitation in advertising under the slogan 'The Rolls-Royce of the Bingo Trade'. The company became well-known at the various exhibitions it attended because of the costumes Frank himself designed for the six sales girls on the stand. At one exhibition Frank overhead two men discussing where to start, with one rejecting the suggestion of the other, saying, 'No, first let's go and see what the Thompson girls are wearing'. The costumes changed every year, ranging from the Thompson tartan to a shimmering, glittering silver.

It was at the ATEI that the company was first approached by overseas bingo operators. It was another challenge to relish. As Frank later recollected, 'A great joy of the job was overcoming the problems of internationalising the market'. It had never been done before, bingo had never been so popular at home or abroad, and with so little competition it was an opportunity with huge potential. Frank threw himself into this new avenue with gusto. He did not confine himself to English-speaking countries, such as Australia and New Zealand, the United States and Canada. He was not only armed with an ability, like his father, to absorb languages, equipping him with enough of several languages to see him through many deals; he also had his mother's gift of mimicry, allowing him to speak each language with the same inflection as the person with whom he was negotiating. 'If it doesn't sound like their language,' he would say, 'they won't even listen.' Tom Clark learned a lot about selling from accompanying Frank on some of his early sales visits overseas. 'He realised,' said Tom, 'that the customer was the company.' For Ray Smith, who also travelled with Frank overseas, 'he was a hell of a salesman'. As at home, the company sold on service, not on price, and a deal was always sealed with a handshake, never a written contract. Frank liked to handle all these enquiries himself. Taking Italy as an example, he quickly learned that the customer always wanted to hear from the man in charge even if there were language difficulties. 'The Italians are going to listen to the man who's the boss even if he's struggling with the language and talking rubbish, because he's the one who's telling the truth.' He disliked having interpreters, finding they interrupted the rhythm of negotiations. His reputation as a communicator would make him welcome wherever he went in the world.

As in the UK, the company eventually offered a complete bingo package to overseas operators. Jim Johnson was given a job by Frank Cronin in 1971 and has been there ever since. Ultimately joining the electronics business, Jim travelled all over the world to set up bingo games, from the United States to Brazil and South Africa. By the early 1970s, noted a newspaper article of the company, Edward Thompson was selling bingo tickets in 17 countries. It was even receiving enquiries from Bulgaria and the USSR. Sending bingo tickets overseas required logistical precision. Too heavy to be sent by air, they had to go by sea, a much longer journey which required careful planning if the tickets were to arrive on time at destinations often at the far side of the globe.

3 'THEY COULD NOT HAVE DONE IT WITHOUT ME' – THE CHANGING FACE OF BINGO

During the 1970s Edward Thompson continued to flourish as club bingo remained popular in the UK and overseas. Frank Cronin also played a significant part in the widespread popularity of a new phenomenon, newspaper bingo, which would have as great an impact on the press as the club game had had on the fortune of the cinema chains a generation earlier. But the industry became much more competitive, the business grew more slowly and in the early 1980s it came under serious financial pressure for the first time following the loss of a major deal which had been anticipated. Partly in response to this, Frank Cronin diversified the company's activities outside bingo, investing in a local paper mill, setting up a mailing division and establishing a match factory. These all had mixed fortunes and the heady days of the 1960s never returned. Frank's sons, Philip and Paddy, both entered the business but Philip would move into on-line gaming, leaving Paddy as managing director in 2007.

Edward Thompson was still the largest producer of bingo tickets in the world. By the late 1970s, the company was making 150 million tickets each week, supplying most major bingo circuits and social clubs in the UK and Ireland, providing draw, tote and raffle tickets. It was also selling electronic random number generators, indicator boards and score boards, playing cards, bingo blowers, sound systems and seating. Although the number of clubs in the UK had fallen, stabilising at around 1,700 until the early 1990s, new clubs being opened were on average much larger than those in use in the mid-1960s. For instance, the first purpose-built club in the north, the Regal Bingo complex, opened in Washington in Tyne & Wear in 1976, cost in excess of £250,000 and seated 1,100 players. New legislation in the 1970s at last legalised national link games and paved the way for even bigger prizes.

Frank was always full of ideas for improving the way things were done. From his brush with academia over combinations for the Top Rank game, he had appreciated how computers made calculations so much easier. When the time and the technology were right, he brought computing into the company. The first computer was fondly known as EMILY. She was, recalled Frank, 'monstrous', occupying much of the top floor of the Richmond Street factory, but capable of calculating in seconds the combinations it had taken days to complete manually. Frank always insisted that technology should work for the business and was always irritated by computer managers telling him how much more the computer could do for him. He was also irritated when they challenged his maths – he fired the first four. Frank himself never touched a computer.

Similarly, the sheer number of tickets produced by the company led Frank to consider whether it was possible to print them more efficiently. He began making sketches of the type of machine he had in mind and began looking for someone to build it at the international printing exhibitions he regularly attended. It was at one of these exhibitions that he finally saw a press which he thought had potential for printing bingo tickets. This was the Cameron belt press, used for the speedy production of mass-market books, which had been around since the late 1960s. Frank came up with a scheme for adapting the belt press, using a pair of endless belts, one slightly longer than the other, both rotating at the same speed. The plates on one belt printed part of the ticket, the plates on the longer belt another part. Thanks to the different lengths of each belt, every ticket was printed with different numbers. Ray Smith had gained a reputation as the man who translated Frank's ideas about printing into practice – 'I never said no to Frank, I always said I would try' – and led the team of engineers from Edward Thompson, in association with engineers from the printing press manufacturers, such as Heidelberg, which constructed the innovative belt-type press. A closed-circuit television system was added to overcome the problem that the machine was too big for the operator to have an overall view. 'It made you that little bit special', remembered Frank, 'in a way that the competition could not stay with you.' There were plans to house the new press in another purpose-built factory in Richmond Street.

Frank was often travelling overseas during the 1970s and

1980s, building up the company's export sales. Occasionally accompanied by senior managers from the company, he always took the lead in negotiations, leaving operations in the UK in the hands of Tom Clark and his colleagues. From 1976 onwards, the company licensed its combinations in Australia through Edward Thompson International. Pat Morrow (later Bevis), Frank's secretary since 1974, remembered how this began when an Australian turned up unannounced one day to see Frank. Frank, who would usually agreed to see anyone who called at the office, met the Australian and the result was an arrangement which lasted for more than 30 years. A commotion was caused in Australia in 1985 when multiple winners were created through a printing error on the bingo tickets, with Ray Smith delivering an apology in the Australian press. But such errors were rare and the company continued to add to the long list of countries it supplied. When Frank decided to make a couple of films for customers, one of which was entitled 'Safety in Numbers', demonstrating why the company's combinations produced only single winners, he made sure commentaries were added in French and Italian. The film was made by Matt Smith, with the assistance of Brian Walsh, and featured incidentally the hands of Ray Brown, showing how to tear a ticket correctly. When it was finished, Frank arranged a visit to the headquarters of Granada in Golden Square in London where the film was shown in the main preview theatre and was well-received.

One of the reasons why the company's export trade proved so successful – and continued to grow, reaching more than 100 countries by 2001 – was another phenomenon in the world of bingo. This was newspaper bingo. It began in the UK, appearing in the national press for the first time in the early 1980s, although it had featured in regional papers several years earlier. Among the first were Scotland's *Sunday Post* in 1972 and the *Sheffield Star* in 1975. It was, noted Frank, 'such a great way of selling papers' because readers had to buy a copy every day to complete the numbers they needed for each game. The fear that it would attract drive existing customers away from the clubs proved false. It was massively popular. When one newspaper decided not to deliver bingo cards in a number of more affluent neighbourhoods, it was deluged with complaints. Eventually the national newspapers contracted bingo mania as well, led by Derek Jameson, the editor of the *Daily Star*, which increased circulation by 35 per cent. *The Sun* quickly followed suit with equal success. Other newspapers were more reluctant but soon succumbed. In just six months in 1981 the popular dailies increased their circulation by more than a half a million copies and their revenue by £6 million. On the other hand, according to one newspaper report, this campaign had cost the participating papers £18-20 million in prizes and promotions. The *Daily Express* introduced the first million-pound jackpot in 1984 and the craze even touched the august *Times*, although the game was altered to fit the paper's upmarket image. Edward Thompson was responsible for the *Express* game. The paper had turned to the company, according to one report in the paper, because its computer-controlled system gave every player a fair chance of winning the jackpot.

At one time or another the company supplied games to almost every major UK national newspaper. Frank met leading figures in the industry who were always keen to find out about this man from Sunderland. As Frank remembered, 'You never get the order unless you've seen the boss or you never go away absolutely certain the job's yours without the approval of the big fella'. Among them were David English, the editor of the *Daily Mail*, and Rupert Murdoch: 'it was "David" and "Frank", and "Frank" and "Rupert"', Frank recalled.

Frank's outstanding numeracy skills always impressed potential customers. Pat Bevis recalled a meeting where executives from the *Daily Mail* described a casino-type game they wanted to introduce. Producing a sheet of paper, Frank immediately began scribbling down the concept and mechanics of the game. He could devise a game within minutes yet talked about it as if it was the easiest thing in the world to do. The newspaper wanted three million game cards printed and Frank quite happily worked out in his head there and then the cost of each sheet. His estimate proved to be accurate almost to the penny.

The impact on the company was immediate. By the end of 1981 Edward Thompson was printing 100 million tickets a day. Ray Brown remembered that the factory recruited an additional 360 staff to cope – 'we were pulling people in from the highways and byways' – taking the total workforce to a record 1,080. Things were so busy, recalled Ray, that 'I virtually lived at the factory for weeks on end'. Ray Smith played a key role in helping to meet this extraordinary demand, providing all the necessary technical expertise, sitting with Frank for hours going through everything. The *Daily Mirror's* biggest promotion, also organised by Edward Thompson, originally involved bingo cards distributed to 15 million households, but proved so successful that a further five million were sent out. 'We've been totally overwhelmed by the demand,' the paper's circulation director was reported as saying. 'The whole country seems to have gone bingo crazy.' In the autumn of 1981 for the *Daily Mirror* alone the company was printing almost 19 million tickets every week. Frank Cronin himself believed that 'bingo is the greatest newspaper promotional device ever used'. The idea may not have originated with him but, as he later said, 'They could not have done it without me'.

Newspaper bingo was hugely successful for Edward Thompson overseas. Frank targeted various newspapers, winning orders in many countries. In 1981 the company was already printing tickets for one hundred different newspapers in 28 countries. Pat Bevis described this period as 'just unbelievable, just so mad, so hectic'. Frank's diary was suddenly choked with appointments. For a time the company employed a French agent and Pat reckoned that she made 50 or 60 visits with Frank to Paris, from airport to office to airport, usually just for the day.

Bingo, claimed Frank, was at least ten times more effective in raising circulation than television advertising. He enjoyed particular success in Italy, with papers such as *Il Tempo* in Rome, *La Nazione* in Florence, *Echo di Bergamo, Il Domani di Bologna* and *Journale di*

Brescia. Newspapers in Poland and Czechoslovakia, Spain and Portugal, Australia and New Zealand, all bought bingo games from Frank Cronin. For Frank, the benefit of newspaper bingo was the value of each sale – the game sold to the *Berliner Zeitung,* for instance, was worth £45,000 (worth almost £200,000 today). Remembering his father's wartime service and the damage wreaked on the business during the Second World War, Frank particularly enjoyed selling his bingo game to the Germans.

Frank Cronin never really cracked the United States although, as Ray Smith remarked, he 'always dreamed about conquering America'. Attending exhibitions on the west coast, he did sell the game to several Indian reservations. Still prepared to take calculated risks, he became involved during the 1980s with a scheme for a million-dollar live televised bingo game. In the end the customer ran out of money. Jim Johnson was despatched to collect a cheque personally from the customer to cover existing debts and did bring one back, although he knew it would be worthless even as it was being written. Jim reflected that 'you could understand the gamble Frank took because if it had come off it would have been huge'. Newspaper bingo gave him the opportunity to reinforce his efforts in the USA. He decided from the outset that he would first visit Las Vegas. 'When I wanted to conquer America, where would you want to go first? Las Vegas. I did a lot of research and development there. I went into each place and played a lot of games so I knew I understood. Most of the information I kept in my head but I picked up a few leaflets and grabbed a few bits of paper. I didn't overdo it. You wanted to avoid standing out.' He would sell games to the *Los Angeles Times,* the *Chicago Tribune* and the *New York Times.*

In retrospect, Frank believes that since the international market opened up by newspaper bingo was too big to be dominated by Edward Thompson, it allowed rivals into the market. The newspapers in any case were reluctant to rely too much on a single supplier. This inadvertently created the first major crisis for the business and the first dip in its financial fortunes since 1959. Frank always believed that once he had shaken hands on a deal, it was certain. In anticipation of fulfilling a contract with the *Daily Mirror*, the company had invested considerable sums in stock, but the order fell through and the paper negotiated a deal with a rival supplier.

This occurred at the same time that the company had already agreed to spend several million pounds on the Cameron press which had not yet been delivered. Left with too much stock, a hole in the production schedule and significant capital expenditure commitments, Edward Thompson was faced with a cashflow problem. It had to borrow money for the first time. This was exacerbated by the success of a rival in taking business away from the company, with annual turnover dropping by a third. Frank found that the increasing number of his rivals were happy to sell on price rather than service. There was no alternative but to lay people off. For a man who had prided himself in providing employment, this was a very difficult time. Paddy Cronin recalled his father would cry himself to sleep every night while Tom Clark remembered how Frank became ill with worry. He was reluctant to take any action which meant people might lose their jobs but allowed Tom Clark to do so. The brunt of the job losses was borne by the many hundreds of part-time workers employed by the company, although some full-time staff were also made redundant and some machinery was sold. Frank was grateful to Tom, telling him, 'Tom, I will never forget you for what you have done here'.

Frank had been thinking how he could sustain the numbers of people he employed even before this crisis had occurred. The workforce was already shrinking as production became increasingly automated. For instance, machines took over the task of inserting millions of bingo cards into envelopes. The first opportunity to create more jobs came by coincidence. Paper had been made in Sunderland since the 1870s and for many years a Canadian company, Domtar, had been running the paper mill in Commercial Road. In 1980 Domtar pulled out and closed the mill, leaving it vacant and up for sale. A year later, as the assets were being sold off, Tom Clark was interested in buying the forklift trucks for the

Richmond Street factory. He asked Frank to go along with him but Frank proved to be captivated by the mill itself. He found himself looking at the existing papermaking machine. 'I walked up and down the machine ... and I kept thinking, "Surely to God there must be something that we can do with that?"'

Making paper was something he knew he had to think through carefully before he made a commitment. But he did want the buildings which would provide valuable storage space for a business which was always in desperate need of it. Frank could see in the mill, a rambling complex of red-brick industrial buildings, the potential not just for producing paper for his own presses but also for providing more jobs. His immediate offer of a million pounds was not taken seriously but later that afternoon the mill managing director, convinced of Frank's sincerity, rang him and a deal was agreed in principle.

The mill was brought back into use during 1982. At first the space was used as an overflow for finishing tickets from Richmond Street. Ray Smith remembered that the buildings could be so cold to work in during the winter that the workers joked they had seen polar bears. Frank became convinced the mill could make money from producing recycled paper collected from the factory and local councils. It was, he remembered, 'a little bit revolutionary at the time'. He bought a big reel-fed press and installed it as part of a multi-million-pound investment programme. As one of the few mills in the country producing recycled paper, the Sunderland Paper Mill, as it was renamed, not only began supplying the company with paper for bingo tickets but also turned out high- class writing and printing papers as well as cheaper computer listing paper. It won customers at home and overseas. Ultimately, employment at the mill went a long way to making up for the lost jobs as the workforce reached a record 1,100.

The match factory was another opportunistic venture which created more jobs. After the *Sunderland Echo* moved into new premises in 1976, Frank bought the former offices in Bridge Street for additional storage space. There was only one other match factory, Bryant & May, in the UK and Frank discovered that most match books were imported from Japan. With smoking still permitted in clubs, he saw an opportunity to add match books to the ancillary goods offered to customers as well as the chance of supplying hotels and restaurants. Production began in 1982 and within a decade the factory had achieved sales of a million pounds and was employing 28 people. The first manager was John Macdonald, who came from Doxford's, the Sunderland shipyard. He had lived in the same street, been to the same school and attended the same church as Frank Cronin. He was later succeeded by Ken Bevis who moved with the business, which traded as Matchmakers International, when it was eventually sold to an Indian company in 2002.

After the sale, the Bridge Street buildings became redundant as Edward Thompson no longer needed it for storage. Frank wondered what on earth he could do with it. His two younger sons, Philip and Paddy, who were now in the business, were in favour of selling the ageing property, but Frank appreciated that the real value lay not in the buildings but in the site, which stood right alongside the river. He believed he could persuade the council to grant planning permission, an aspiration which met with some scepticism. Frank tells the story how he set out to convince councillors that he wanted the planned development to resemble a ship in tribute to Sunderland's shipbuilding past – 'and the council loved it'. As a result, instead of thousands for the old buildings, the company received several millions for the sale of the site.

There were other opportunities for job creation. Ray Brown had persuaded Frank that the company should invest in its own envelope-making machinery, which would not only meet the needs of the company but also open up sales to external customers. Eventually the company was operating several machines and also added envelope-inserting equipment. This led Ray to convince Philip Cronin that the company should set up its own mailing division. Started with machines bought cheaply from another business, adding polythene wrapping followed by high-speed personalisation, the division became a profitable part of the business.

The contracts division also continued to develop, supplying scoring systems developed by Wearside Electronics to the world snooker championship, international tennis tournaments and national athletics stadiums. On the bingo side, one of the major contracts completed by the division was the bingo auditorium in Sun City in South Africa.

For Frank, all these additional activities helped Edward Thompson to recover from the crisis of the early 1980s, although there were those who felt that diversification stretched the limited management resources of the business. The company also maintained its leading position as a supplier of bingo tickets. When the National Bingo Game was launched in 1986, the combinations and tickets were all supplied by Edward Thompson. Technology made it possible to link by computer 500 clubs playing for an initial national jackpot of £50,000 plus several smaller regional jackpots. Until the introduction of the National Lottery in 1994 this was the biggest computer-controlled game in the UK. The challenge met by Edward Thompson was supplying tickets to so many different sites simultaneously, a task fulfilled which sustained the company's reputation for service. The company's hundred-strong delivery fleet distributed 650,000 tickets every 24 hours.

But things were changing. The fad for newspaper bingo was waning and the popularity of bingo clubs was falling. It had become a mature market. By the early 1990s the number of licensed clubs had fallen below a thousand – partly accounted for by the closure of the traditional working men's clubs – while the industry was consolidating, dominated by the larger chains which accounted for two-thirds of a market estimated to be worth £1.4 billion every year and employing 35,000 people. In 1992 Top Rank remained the largest UK bingo chain, with 147 clubs, but the name was on the verge of disappearing in favour of the Mecca brand, following Top Rank's acquisition of Mecca Leisure in 1990. It was closely followed by Gala, created from the merger of the Coral and

Granada clubs after the takeover of Granada by Bass Leisure in 1991. Gala grew steadily, gobbling up other small chains, such as Ritz and Riva, eventually overtaking Mecca. To maintain existing customers, attract a new generation of younger bingo players and sustain revenues, the operators invested heavily during the 1990s in purpose-built clubs, modern technology and bigger prizes. It was Gala which introduced the UK's first digital touch-screen bingo club in Peterborough in 1992. The Super Nova National Game launched in 1993 offered a maximum prize of £95,000 while Top Rank laid out £29 million every year in prize money through the National Game. Within this shrinking market – and the same decline was seen overseas – Edward Thompson retained a significant share. Offering a comprehensive package from tickets to complete club refurbishments, the company made sure it kept up with technological developments in the bingo world.

By the early 1990s the company was turning over nearly £30 million and overseas sales were still growing. By 1993 the company had customers in 60 countries, covering Europe, Australasia, the Far East and North America, and the company was awarded the Queen's Award for Exports. In the same year the company had designed, renovated and supervised the opening of two clubs in Moscow. While Frank Cronin's senior managers, Tom Clark, Ray Smith and Ray Brown, were still integral to the running of the business, Frank was now working alongside his two younger sons, Philip and Paddy. Philip, appointed managing director, had many new ideas for the business, not all of which found favour with his father. In particular they disagreed over the future of the paper mill, which Philip wanted to close, an issue which led to his departure from the company. Frank proved his point by securing the future of the mill for another decade.

By the new millennium, the company's sales had reached £40 million annually (compared with £750,000 in 1965). The business was split roughly equally between bingo, the paper mill and promotional printing. An article in *Printing World* in September 2000 was headed 'Master of the Full House – Frank Cronin and his worldwide niche market in bingo printing'. The company continued to manage games for national newspapers at home and abroad. The article noted that 'by handling the entire management of these games as an independent contractor, Edward Thompson guarantees a scrupulously run operation with a crystal clear fair result'. This was absolutely critical since contracts for newspaper games stipulated that the supplier had to make up the difference if any single game yielded more than one million-pound prizewinner. But Frank Cronin's tried and tested combinations remained sound. Another reason for the company's resilience was the willingness of the workforce to work flexibly, moving from department to department and machine to machine, gaining wider experience and skills, rewarded by a profit-related bonus scheme. The company also continued to invest in printing technology. The latest tailor-made Sanden nine-colour rotary letter-press machine from Canada, costing £1.25 million, was turning out scratch-cards for Kenya. By now Kenya was just one of more than a hundred countries, including Brazil and Bolivia, Thailand and Vietnam, China and Japan, where Edward Thompson had customers, a significant increase over the previous decade. The company was also printing the almost unbelievable number of one billion bingo game cards every week.

Several million pounds had been invested in the paper mill. Three hundred people working triple shifts turned out 600 tonnes of 100 per cent recycled paper every week. But eventually even Frank was unable to keep the mill running. What killed it was an end to the cheap energy on which it depended to make a profit. When energy costs soared, it ceased to be viable. By late 2005 energy was costing the mill £2.5 million, compared with sales of £10 million. A phased closure was announced and the mill finally stopped production in April 2006. Frank stood and shook hands with every employee.

Bingo too remained under pressure, following greater regulation, higher taxation and the imposition of the smoking ban from July 2007. By 2000 the number of people playing bingo every week in the UK had declined to five million, compared with the 14 million members signed up in the early 1960s, and this figure had dropped to three million by 2010, with the number of licensed clubs falling to less than 700. But the game adapted to changing circumstances. The major chains, such as Gala, now the company's major customer, still saw money in bingo – in 2004 the chain paid £18 million for a modern profitable club in Basingstoke. The clubs continued to offer bigger and bigger prizes, with the first £1 million game in 2002, and the first bingo millionaire in 2007.

The new phenomenon was on-line bingo. The first on-line site in the UK was launched in 2003. Although the clubs feared it would have a detrimental impact on them, it seems that on-line players have been encouraged to join clubs as well. Just as Frank had seized the opportunity offered by the explosion in commercial bingo, his son Philip saw the potential in on-line bingo, leaving the company to develop his own business, first in partnership with the *Sun* newspaper, and then under the name of Tombola. Frank too realised the greater variety and convenience offered by the new medium. Tombola has developed just as rapidly as Edward Thompson did in the early 1960s and has become the biggest on-line bingo site. Bingo in the on-line version has become fashionable with newspapers again, with several of the popular tabloids establishing their own sites, as have most of the commercial bingo chains. This new world was opening up just as Frank was moving out of the business as he reached the age of 70. Several of those who had helped him to build up Edward Thompson into one of the leading names in bingo worldwide, including Tom Clark, Ray Smith and Ray Brown, had preceded him into retirement. He had had a huge impact on what was still the second most popular pastime in the UK by helping it to spread its popularity and keep it relevant to the changing world. As Tom Clark noted, 'Bingo became what it is because of what Frank Cronin did'.

4 'PURE ENTREPRENEURSHIP' – THE BUSINESSMAN

In many ways Frank Cronin was a typical entrepreneur. He could spot an opportunity and exploit it. He was unafraid of taking risks but the risks he took were carefully calculated. He was financially prudent. He was stimulated by challenges to discover solutions and could adapt to change. He liked to be in control and made all the important decisions. He respected his staff and was never aloof. He worked hard and at a furious pace. He had a flair for communication and a passion for selling. His negotiating skills were outstanding and his mathematical skills gave him a unique advantage. Where Frank differed from the traditional entrepreneur was in his driving conviction that the business existed primarily to serve his customers and his workforce.

Frank lived and breathed the business. He found it endlessly enjoyable and satisfying. 'There's been great fun in my life. I've enjoyed every minute of it. I've never been bored in my life. The challenge was to create things that nobody else was doing, to go one step further.' Business gave purpose to his life, along with his family, although the latter sometimes felt that they came second in Frank's affections. He had a huge appetite for work, with his working week regularly exceeding 60 hours. He believed there was a pay-off from all this effort — 'the harder I work, the luckier I get'. His secretary, Pat Bevis, witnessed his punishing schedule at first hand. She was expected to be on call at all times. For instance, she might be told late in the afternoon that the next morning she would be flying with him to France.

The business was so much part of him, he had grown up with it, he had expanded it so fast, that it never occurred to him that management was a subject which could be taught. It was simply something he lived. He could never understand the need for management courses although he never quite closed his mind to the possibility he might learn something from attending one. In Frank's early years, remembered Tom Clark, he could be 'cavalier' with rules and regulations, but he was also 'fearless', a man who 'did not look for problems, he never saw failure as a prospect'. He was ideally suited to the industry for he had a gambling instinct, a willingness to take risks and chance failure. Frank believed that 'the man who had never made a mistake has not lived'. 'If you were right, you were right,' he said, 'but if you were wrong, you were wrong, but you'd already made your decision, and you made your fair share of wrong decisions.' But the risks he took were always finely calculated, as they would be from a man who devised virtually fail-safe bingo combinations. 'I always worked out the effect of anything I wanted to do on everything else I was doing ... I would try and see if it worked ... I never rushed at things. I always had a toe in the water. Toe in the water is a good policy – try it first, don't go mad.'

Frank liked to be in control. Quite simply, said Brian Walsh, 'He *was* Edward Thompson'. His son Philip remarked that his father 'was the finance director, he was the sales director, he was the head of product development; he had operational managers, he had operational sales managers, but those guys were responsible for getting the work out of the door, for getting the jobs done. What they weren't involved with was what was going to be the next thing.' Frank, observed his son, probably thought that he was the best person in every department within the company. Although Tom Clark, Ray Smith, Ray Brown and Brian Walsh all became directors of the business, they did not exercise the influence which usually came with the appointment. Tom Clark recalled that when he was first made a director, he was called 'administrative and technical director', but it was merely a title and did not even bring a rise in salary. With directors given responsibility but little authority, Edward Thompson, Tom believed, was 'not a normal company'. Ray Smith described the position of director at the company as nothing more than 'a glorified manager'. The directors hardly ever met together because Frank regarded most meetings as a waste of time and a meeting, however uncommon, never occurred without him. While the directors knew a great deal about their own area of the business, the only person with a complete overview was Frank, and it was something he rarely shared. He accumulated the information he wanted from one-to-one conversations in his office or a few passing words in the corridor. He became known as 'the Scarlet Pimpernel' because he was usually missing from his office. He disliked being alone and preferred to wander around the factory, picking up information. Each director would talk to him about their own part of the business but rarely with other colleagues and Frank never asked them to make presentations. There were no general discussions about sales strategies or product development. Frank would tell people exactly what he wanted them to do, at which he was very good. This was usually the only reason board meetings took place. Sometimes voices would be raised. Tom Clark recalled that there were some 'unbelievable rows' between them but Frank never bore a grudge, 'there was never any spitting dummies out'. Whenever there was a difference of opinion, Frank would convince people he was right and he usually won. Madge Johnson remembered he liked to say, 'Trust in me, believe in me and know that I am right'. He was often referred to as 'God' because so often what he said would happen, did.

While managers worked within confined boundaries, and were permitted little flexibility, Frank would say that he rarely interfered in what they did from day to day. From his point of view, he appointed capable men to carry out their duties competently in a specific part of the organisation and as long as they were doing a good job he left them alone. But it was always quite clear that, as Brian Walsh noted, Frank 'was the only man who said how the company worked'. This could be frustrating for managers and some of them found that the best way of persuading him to accept an idea was to suggest that it had been his in the first place. Frank would claim that he allowed his managers this ruse because the idea truly was his and he wanted them to think it was theirs.

While persuading others to do what he wanted came naturally to Frank, it was unusual for anyone, recalled Madge Johnson, to persuade him to do anything he was set against. If they tried, he could become bloody-minded and awkward. Once he had made up his mind, Tom Clark discovered, it was virtually impossible to make him change it. This was all part of Frank's insistence on retaining control. If Teresa, for instance, rang the office in the early evening to try to persuade Frank to come home, he would deliberately leave even later than usual because, as Pat Bevis remarked, 'it had to be his decision'. When Pat booked a flight or train tickets for him, Frank would insist, 'I don't want to go on that one!', and 'unarrange' things. Pat would often return to her desk, kick the desk panel and throw the date stamp in frustration. Frank knew the effect he had on her but always appreciated the way she filled her role as his personal assistant – 'she's got some of a wife's role in bullying you to get you to do what she wants you to do'.

Ray Brown felt that Frank liked to think he could delegate but found it difficult not to have a finger in every pie. Tom Clark also believed that Frank tried to delegate, he was just not very good at it. Tom recounted how in the absence of a formal buying system, with department heads ordering goods as and when they were needed, Frank kept things in check by scrutinising every invoice and signing every cheque. The only other person Frank allowed to sign cheques on behalf of the company was his father. Pat Bevis recalled that wherever she went with Frank, on trains, in planes, in cars and taxis, waiting in stations or in airports, they would always be writing cheques. Many a train journey to and from London was occupied entirely by writing cheques. He would even write cheques as a spectator at his sons' sports days.

An exception to the limited degree of delegation Frank was happy to concede was his willingness to place the day-to-day management of the whole business in the hands of Tom Clark whenever he was out of the country. 'He was in charge when I went out.' Frank always took the lead in international sales, believing winning export contracts at the right price was one of the most difficult things to achieve. He had to leave someone else in charge of the business. He trusted Tom, down to earth and intelligent, steeped in the traditions of the company, who would ultimately become deputy managing director. Despite what some thought, Frank understood the importance of having managers who were capable of assuming responsibility in his absence. He could go away knowing that 'all the guys were playing the game properly'. Frank admitted that delegation was not something which came easily. 'I miss it, you know, the actual hands-on job. But there was a limit to how much you could do. It was the team.'

This was probably why Frank almost always preferred to make senior appointments from within the business. 'I don't like the idea of bringing Joe Bloggs in and him telling other people how to do their job when he doesn't know what they're doing.' He also believed that employing people whose backgrounds you knew something about was better than employing those about whom you knew nothing. He considered personality was as important as any other attributes in his managers. 'When you had your managers, you had some of them who weren't warm enough to be ideal for me, but they functioned … I believed that "Love Thy Neighbour" always worked better. A good manager shouldn't need to be shouting out about the place all the time. If a guy's not doing the job, it could be because he's clumsy or something, you can go and help him to correct it; to shout at him is a mistake, because then you'll just make him worse.'

Frank believed in this approach because it was one he had always successfully followed himself. He had seen it in the way his father treated the handful of staff he employed during the 1950s. This had not only won their respect but strengthened their commitment, with most of them serving many years with the company. Throughout his life Frank has valued people above anything else. Tom Clark observed that he rarely talked about profit. 'Money didn't mean anything to Frank.' As Frank told a journalist in 1981, 'People are more important than money. However rich you are, you can still only wear one suit at a time'. As a child, Frank had seen the misery unemployment had brought for many thousands of local men and women. That was why giving people employment was always such a priority and gave him so much satisfaction. 'I always tried to give them a job for life.' For Frank, as his son Paul later reflected, 'Dad's idea was that his job was to find work for his staff and if he did a good job at that, there would be some money left to look after his and kids.' 'Money really wasn't it,' commented Philip Cronin. 'The drive was to solve problems for other people so they would pay him money so he could pay his staff money so they could take it home and look after their families.' Edward Thompson, reflected Brian Walsh, was 'never a hire and fire company'. Frank made a point of interviewing almost every applicant for every vacancy and always tried to find out something about each of them. The worst times in his business life were when the company had to make employees redundant. 'Frank never wanted to make people redundant,' said Madge Johnson. 'He always got somebody else to do it. He only ever employed people.' Rather than dismiss someone if they were proving unsatisfactory, he generally preferred to move them into a new role. For him the great satisfaction of developing the paper mill was creating several hundred jobs. He was particularly proud of an award received by the company for employing disabled staff.

For Frank, keeping people motivated was the key to the company's prosperity. The company was often working to very tight deadlines, which frequently meant that staff were asked to work long hours in order to meet the delivery times and standards of service on which Edward Thompson had built its success. Frank believed it was important that there were always enough staff with the right attitude to deliver service to the customers. The single most important stimulus to motivating people was the bonus scheme Frank introduced very early on. His eldest son Stephen recalled that 'Dad's greatest reward was how many people he employed and how many people he gave a Christmas bonus to'. Frank saw all sorts of advantages in the bonus scheme. 'A bonus,' he said, 'is vital. Why should they work their socks off and you take all the money out?' He believed it made it easier to maintain efficiency since a bonus could be withdrawn for carelessness. It made the foreman's job easier – 'you don't have to shout at anybody ... they know that if the work gets out and the money comes in, they get a share'. And it encouraged staff to work as a team and 'feel part of the company'. The original scheme was quite complex, and based on the random allocation of points, but it generated enthusiasm among many workers. This was partly because the basic wage was never regarded as being particularly generous at Edward Thompson. On his return to the factory after an overseas sales visit, Frank was often waylaid by workers eager to know how many new orders he had brought back. In the early years Frank would also reward record production weeks with gifts of cigarettes for the men and tights for the women. A more objective basis for bonuses was eventually introduced by Ray Brown, following a work study exercise, resulting in the allocation of bonus according to the rate at which work was completed. It was a change which Frank was persuaded to accept only with difficulty.

He appreciated the importance of praising staff, especially those who learned from their mistakes. 'Somebody who makes a mistake that costs you money, later on when he gets the job right, it's well worth going across and telling him it was a fabulous job because you're not going to get the problem again. Mistakes do happen, that's the truth.' As much as anything he loved walking through the offices and around the factory talking to staff. 'Frank,' remembered Brian Walsh, 'used to get out of his office and wander around – he knew who everyone was and he knew everything that was going on.' 'How are you doing, bonny lad?' was his typical greeting. He was very approachable and his office door was always open to staff. Just as he made a point of knowing everyone by their first name, so they all knew him as Frank. (Teresa never thought this was quite right, believing that 'Mr Cronin' would have shown more respect for Frank as their employer.) He believed that 'if "Love Thy Neighbour" permeates the whole place, everyone wants to get things right'. Linda Holden felt that 'there was a great camaraderie, we were all close-knit … we used to laugh all the time … it was different and it was vibrant … every day was different'. Madge Johnson considered that Frank's approach created a warmth throughout the company which made so many people happy to come to work and spent their working lives with Edward Thompson. The people at the company, she said, were 'my extended family ... there was a feeling of family ... you just loved to go to work'. Staff stayed so long, said Brian Walsh, not because the pay was particularly good but because of 'the very hospitable side of the company'. Pat Bevis recalled how 'we used to work hard but we had a very good laugh as well'.

Frank was never averse to the unions but believed they were most effective where employees were being exploited – 'where management is top quality, the union is irrelevant'. At Edward Thompson, it was possible for workers to earn well above the union rates when the bonus was taken into account. Industrial relations were usually harmonious. One exception occurred in the early 1970s when it was still possible for workers at one company to go out on strike in sympathy with workers elsewhere. When the van drivers at Edward Thompson threatened to take sympathetic strike action, Frank was uncomprehending. Disrupting distribution would threaten the quality of service and good customer relations on which he had built up the business. Displaying the rarely seen steely side of his character, he told the drivers that if necessary he himself would drive a van and if that happened they would no longer have jobs with the company. When Teresa, his wife, appeared that morning with Frank's packed lunch, the drivers knew he was serious. They stayed at work.

While the company offered numerous benefits, from a subsidised canteen to staff loans, Frank never established an effective pension scheme. He tried and abandoned several limited schemes and then the financial crisis of the early 1980s made a company-wide scheme unaffordable. Instead, the decision was left to the individual and, as Madge Johnson recalled, advice was given to those willing to pay into personal pension schemes. For some of those who had worked closest with Frank, the lack of a pension when they retired was a bitter pill to swallow after many years of loyal service.

Frank's 'Love Thy Neighbour' principle was applied not only to staff but also to customers and suppliers, just as Frank had seen his father do. 'In commercial terms, the neighbour is all the people you work with, the neighbour is all the people you buy from and the neighbour is all the people you sell to. If you're good mates with your suppliers, you're going to get the best prices, and if you're good mates with your customers, you're going to get your sales up, and if you're not good mates with your staff, you're bloody stupid, because they're not going to graft when you turn your back.' The only weakness of this approach was that Frank instinctively trusted people. Sometimes they let him down, for instance, a number of agents whom he appointed overseas. Frank was a man without enemies and a man who never spoke a word against anyone. One of his frequent sayings was 'If you have nothing good to say, don't say anything'. Neil Wright, a friend, remembered Frank's advice that you should trust someone if you believed they had more good than bad in them.

Frank's control extended to the financial management of the business. Few of the directors knew either how the business was performing overall or whether their own division was making money. There were never any budgets, let alone management accounts. When Philip Cronin analysed one section of the business and discovered it was unprofitable, his father was strongly opposed to revealing the situation to the director in charge. As far as he was concerned such news would act only as a disincentive to the achievement of the basic targets set for the division. With his mathematical facility, Frank himself was able to carry a running assessment of the company's financial health in his head, telling Philip that accountancy after all was only about addition and subtraction. Tom Clark recalled how Frank had a simple method for establishing whether the business was making any money – sales less purchases and wages equalled profit – and kept a close eye on cashflow.

For many years he was able to do without a financial director. He never liked accountants even though his brother was a qualified accountant who would later come to work for him. He had, observed Brian Walsh, seen too often the damage they had done to firms within the bingo industry. Madge Johnson remembered attending one accountancy seminar with Frank where he became increasingly agitated. Finally he could contain himself no longer, stood up, made it quite clear to the whole room how he felt about what was being said and then walked out, leaving a bemused Madge to follow after him. 'The businessman's role,' said Frank, 'is making the money and the accountant's role is sweeping up after him. But they would come in and think they could tell you how to run the business.' His antipathy was not helped by the fact that one accountant he recruited falsely claimed to be qualified and another was dishonest. Others were junior appointments, often still studying for their qualification, and providing information for the auditors rather than management. Madge Johnson was the one person Frank came to rely upon for the financial administration of the business. Joining the company in her twenties, she had ten years' experience before she was appointed financial controller in 1977, becoming administration director six years later, with responsibility for the finance team.

Frank had a conservative approach to money, always spending only what the business was earning, insisting that the business should always own rather than lease its assets, and refusing for years to borrow money. As Ray Brown recalled, 'Frank was always a very careful person, he would not go into debt for anything'. He had a reputation for watching the pennies. As Jim Johnson remembered, 'We always had a thing about saving money so Frank would often share a room with me when we were away'. Salesmen, recalled Brian Walsh, never enjoyed generous expenses – in 1966 one guinea, or 21 shillings, had to cover an evening meal and overnight accommodation. Frank also refused to pay for company cars which might antagonise customers. All the salesmen drove Minis – with his long legs, Brian Walsh found this very difficult, and once ended up driving beneath the tailgate of a lorry when his feet slipped off the pedals. For many years Frank's deputy, Tom Clark, drove around in a Hillman Imp. Yet Frank was never ungenerous. When the firm attended exhibitions, Frank made sure everyone went out together in the evenings. Jim can remember eating in the restaurant at the top of what was then the Post Office Tower or visiting Stringfellow's nightclub. Frank later summed up his attitude towards money. 'The good Lord gave me far more money than I ever needed. It was just one of those things. I never was short of cash. And yet I never overcharged anybody, I took a margin always, which you needed to buy your replacement stock. But I never pushed it, because if you pushed it, you started losing work, because somebody else would come in and take it off you ... If you're happy with a margin, it works, and if it works, and the company grows bigger, a margin which is not a lot of money at the start becomes a fortune.'

He was shrewd when dealing with bankers. Tom Clark recalled one occasion when the bank insisted on reducing the level of the company's overdraft facility. Frank refused to accept this decision and was eventually invited to the bank's London headquarters to put his case, accompanied by Tom. Halfway through the negotiations the bank's directors wined and dined their guests in the bank's own restaurant which looked out across the capital. It was an excellent meal but Frank, the lifelong teetotaller, remained utterly sober. When discussions resumed, Frank pressed home his advantage and came away from the meeting with the bank having agreed to increase his facility.

In his prime Frank's control of the business was almost superhuman. He never wasted a moment yet always gave the impression of being relaxed. He kept fit by playing squash three times a week and eventually built his own court reached from the back of his office. His sons, growing up during the 1960s and 1970s, thought their father was invincible. His youngest son Paddy described how his father 'was like a whirlwind when he was at work'. He was also struck by how positive he was all the time, a quality he would later strive to emulate. While Frank did make concessions to being hands-on, as he began travelling more frequently overseas, they never fundamentally altered the way he had run the business. His directors still remained in day-to-day charge of their own parts of the business with little involvement in deciding its future direction.

Strategy was never really a major consideration for Frank. He was an opportunist, seizing the moment as it arose, an approach which had transformed the company. He later described the way in which the business developed. 'It was funny, all the way along what you did was you were presented with circumstances, you made your decision, forgot about it, and got on with the job. You didn't really go in for in-depth analysis.' Yet although he never mapped out the firm's strategy, Frank always had a clear view of where he was going. Frank, his brother Jim remarked, was so focused on the business, he often noticed little outside it. The incredible growth of the company in its heyday owed everything to Frank's sharp mind. His son Philip came to appreciate this in particular after he had completed the Advance Management Program at Harvard Business School in 2002. He realised that the course was teaching him things which his father had been putting into practice for years. And when he returned to Sunderland, he appreciated even more his father's grasp of detail, his rapid insight into new ventures, his capacity for lateral thinking and his ability to sum up quickly the essence of any issue. He was always questioning, always absorbing new information. Pat Bevis recalled how you could sense Frank's mind ticking over all the time, always alert to opportunities, quick to pick up lessons learned from others. His brother Jim pointed out how Frank learned from his mistakes but never dwelt on them and soon forgot all about them.

Although Frank placed huge importance on providing jobs, he never forgot that what drove employment was winning orders. The same talents he applied to motivating the workforce in the factory he also used with customers. 'His lust for sales,', said Jim Johnson, 'was phenomenal.' He was fearless in opening up new territories. He rarely researched a market and was happy just to fly out to a new country and begin selling. Frank was a supreme salesman because he was a great communicator. 'All of life is selling,' he told one of his sons. He believed that he had been born knowing how to negotiate a deal. He was doing deals in the school playground. 'I was even negotiating over conkers at school, how to negotiate the one that was going to last longest from the fella who had it.' His natural charm was a huge asset in making customers feel comfortable. 'You don't win by beating people over the head ... if you have a degree of love, and a degree of humility, it tends to work in the end ... it's basic common sense so why make life harder?' He believed strongly that 'the biggest thing of all is to communicate love ... love creates belief in the other person'. He always sought to empathise with customers. He could adopt the accent of the people with whom he was talking. His second son Paul recalled how, apart from bringing back presents from his trips away, 'the other thing he would always bring back was another accent'. He also tried hard to blend in with his surroundings, whether in other regions of the UK or in distant countries overseas. 'Don't stand out like a sore thumb,' Frank would say, '... the fitting in and merging is important.' So too was his gift for languages. He knew enough to make a difference in a long list of languages, from French, German and Italian to Japanese and Swahili. 'I never learned any of them well and I never ever went anywhere to learn them ... it was a necessity.' It was said of his French, for instance, that Frank only ever spoke in the present tense, but he had a great vocabulary and was never afraid of beginning a conversation. His ability to capture an accent perfectly would often mislead others into thinking he was a fluent speaker. When he was travelling to Japan for the first time, he asked his brother John, who had served with the army there, to advise him on the necessary cultural and linguistic etiquette. Frank always believed strongly in giving proper consideration to customers wherever they were from.

All this was part of making it as easy as possible for customers to do business with him. That was why Frank never said no to customers. It was his job to find a way to give them whatever they wanted. 'We were always market-led,' recalled Frank. 'Whatever needed to be done, we would do.' That was also why Frank always charged overseas customers a price inclusive of freight because he never wanted anything to deter them from doing business with a UK company. He welcomed customers bringing him their problems and salesmen were encouraged to do everything they could to help customers find solutions. This service ethos cemented long-term customer relationships. The company's most important customer today is the Gala chain of bingo clubs for which Edward Thompson has acted as sole supplier for many years. The strong relationship Frank built up with Gala's managing director, John Kelly, was key to this in the earliest days. Building a business based on service made it possible to charge a premium price. Frank's approach brought Edward Thompson not only the largest share of the market but also the biggest margins in the industry.

By the time Frank finally stepped down from the business in 2003, Edward Thompson had been at the top of the tree for five decades. As his son Stephen observed, Frank 'had made everything … Edward Thompson was created by my Dad'. Tom Clark, who probably worked more closely with Frank than anyone, described watching him in action as 'pure entrepreneurship'. It seems the perfect summary for Frank Cronin the businessman.

PART 3
THE FAMILY MAN

Family was as important to Frank Cronin as business, even if the latter sometimes seemed to claim much more of his time. His sons remembered how their mother, frustrated as Frank embarked on yet another overseas visit, would often march them to the front door as their father walked to his car. 'Do you see that man there?,' she would say pointedly. 'That man is your father.' Frank did spend a lot of time away from his family, and often seemed absorbed by business even when he was with them, but home was a vital part of his life. It was a haven away from work, where Teresa had the final say, and Frank played a supporting role. The couple complemented each other superbly, and without Teresa taking charge of his domestic arrangements, Frank would have found life very difficult. They had their differences, which is hardly surprising, given their different priorities, but their relationship was a close and loving one. This too was the nature of their own relationship with their four boys, Stephen, Paul, Philip and Patrick, even though their father sometimes seemed to appear only fleetingly.

Frank himself had been brought up in a loving home. He had been close to his mother, whose absence he felt deeply after her death at an early age, and he became very close to his father. John Louis revelled in his son's success and loved accompanying him to exhibitions. The two shared an office for many years and John Louis came into work regularly until shortly before his death in 1979. Frank gave him a driver, Charlie, who would take him from his home to the office or wherever else he wanted to go. For many years he was the only other person apart from Frank with responsibility for signing the company's cheques. Frank looked upon his father as 'a gentle giant, kind, thoughtful and helpful', a description echoed by Frank's sons about their own father. Frank remembered how his father 'tried his best to make us grow up good boys but through words, he used words, nothing else'. Jim Cronin recalled that his father had three interests in life, his business, his family and the Church, and these too became Frank's interests. As Jim recalled, 'Faith was very important in the home'.

Frank and Jim became particularly close as brothers. Frank's elder brother, John, moved away, although the two became closer in later life when John returned to work for Frank. Jim too would move away from home, firstly to train to be a priest, and later when he became a missionary in Kenya. Frank would often visit him in Africa, sometimes taking his father. He remembered how they walked into the bush, accompanied by a Masai armed with a spear – 'We actually walked amongst the lions which was bloody scary.' He was fascinated by Africa and loved the welcoming, all-embracing and enthusiastic outlook of the local people. Frank was also very generous in supporting Jim's work, helping towards the development of a local school. Jim finally returned to the UK in 2005 and in 2009 celebrated his golden jubilee as a priest, of which his brother was very proud. He is, said Frank, 'a very homely priest'. Today, says Jim, Frank is 'the closest friend I have in the world' and the two men still regularly take five or six-mile walks along the coast close to their homes.

The closest relationship in Frank's life was with Teresa. She gave up work when the couple started a family, to which she devoted the rest of her life. They began their married life at 10 Appleforth Avenue, in Grangetown, bought for £425 before they were married, where their first three sons were born, Stephen in 1956, Paul in 1960 and Philip in 1964. After Philip's birth, the family was looking for somewhere larger and found 97 Whitburn Road in Cleadon. Bought in 1964 for less than £6,000, this was a terraced house with a lovely back garden, about a hundred yards long, ideal for young children. Here Frank and Teresa's last son, Paddy, was born in 1965. Eventually the family crossed the road to a large detached house at

60, Whitburn Road, where they remained. Paul recalled that before the family moved into the house, he and Stephen spent the night there, sleeping on a mattress in what is now the dining room – unaware that later on his parents would look in to make sure the boys were all right. It was Teresa who influenced the changes the couple made to the house, particularly the large wrap-around conservatory. Her request to the architect for 'three greenhouses in the roof' filled the space with light.

As a married couple, their relationship was a traditional one, with Frank cast in the role of breadwinner, and Teresa as home-maker. At home, as Paddy Cronin recalled, 'My Dad was absolutely useless when it came to looking after anybody.' The only dish he knew how to cook with any confidence was sausage and mash which he had learned when he was in the scouts. He was never very domesticated. 'The nearest towel rack,' remembered Paddy, 'was the floor and you would walk around the house and there would be discarded towels everywhere.' Frank's usual routine would be to arrive home from work, make himself comfortable in his large Parker Knoll armchair and ignore everyone, perfectly content with his bowl of fruit and complete control over the television. He went through the ritual of holding every segment of his orange up to the light to check for pips and depositing the peel on the floor. Taking himself upstairs to the bathroom, he would spend hours in the bath which had a built-in thermostat to maintain a constant temperature. As Paddy observed, 'He vegged out and switched off and my mother took control'. Although Frank had the role of head of the household, it was little more than a ceremonial position, with Teresa wielding the real influence. Frank remembered that 'Teresa almost ran a protection racket to make sure that they didn't worry Dad if he'd had a busy day'.

She encouraged Frank in everything he did and he always sought her opinion. 'She was a lady with her own mind,' said Frank. 'She was very much her own woman … she propped me up, she always had an honest opinion … she was a definite team member.' She too was a convinced Catholic and her faith was probably stronger than Frank's for much of her life. The family attended mass without fail every Sunday morning. They were never allowed to arrive early but would have to drive around again; and they always sat at the back. Paddy Cronin remembered a font for holy water by the front door of the house, which later fell into disuse, as well as statues of Joseph and Mary, the latter eventually losing her hands after being dropped several times.

While Teresa's faith began to fail towards the end of her life, Frank's remained fairly constant. 'Dad never lost it,' said Paul Cronin, 'but he never had it as strongly as Mum.' Frank once told Stephen that his faith was based on 'a percentage belief', a rational approach for a man who made his living from calculating risk, and a way of reconciling his belief in the logical and the scientific with his belief in God. Ultimately for Frank, it would all come down to one thing – 'We only need the fourth commandment. The love element is the biggest of all. "Love Thy Neighbour" is positive, it's real and in your face [while] God is somewhere a long way away.'

Teresa's strength of character comes through even in the smallest of details. She was, remembered Frank, 'a lovely dancer' who found herself partnered by 'this great big hunk with two left feet'. She rose to the challenge – 'She bashed me into shape ... The magic to me was that I had this lady who floated in my arms ... and there would be a certain shove on the shoulder until I got the thing right ... I was given a set of physical instructions as we went round the floor.' Jim Cronin believed that 'she had more street-cred than Frank had'. She was a very sociable and hospitable person with the ability to talk to anyone. The Cronin home was regularly filled with groups of her friends. She was an outstanding hostess and loved giving dinner parties. Although she could be crippled by nerves beforehand, she would, said her son Stephen, 'sparkle like a diamond for the rest of the night'. 'Mum', said Paul, 'could light up a room when she walked into it.' In any social situation, she was a shining star, energetic, effervescent, outgoing. She was always immaculately dressed, unlike Frank, for whom clothes were relatively unimportant. (Neil Wright called Frank 'the Egyptian detective' after his habit of wearing the same white suit. A white suit combined with Kangaroo trainers would become one of Frank's trademarks in later life. Madge Johnson recalled Frank 'never gave tuppence for his appearance', once turning up for a meeting with the bank in tracksuit bottoms and trainers.) For Frank, Teresa's confidence was invaluable since, despite his natural charm and warmth, he could be rather shy in social situations unrelated to business. He was happy to hide behind her and retreat into the background. Paul said his father loved to watch her in full flow at a party 'but he didn't need [company] anything like as much as she did'. Teresa never had anything less than complete confidence in Frank. They did not always see eye to eye and they did have their arguments – Paul remembered his mother once kicking his father sharply on the shins – but neither of them held grudges and they almost always made up before the end of the day.

For the boys, home life revolved around their mother, with their father hovering like a satellite in the background. Frank was a benign presence, whose almost imperturbable tolerance and understanding were usually ruffled only by Paul. As a boy, Paul, remembered brother Paddy, Paul 'could try the patience of a saint'. Once, as the family were just about to leave in the car, Frank blew up with Paul. Both of them leapt out of the car, with Frank brandishing one of his shoes, chasing his son round and round the car, with Paul always just out of reach. Their mother would occasionally fall back on using their father as a threat – 'I'll tell your dad' – but, as Paddy noted, 'My Dad was lovely and never did anything nasty to us.' When the boys were younger, although Frank was often late home from work, he would always sing them to sleep in his soothing baritone voice. Stephen's song was 'The Old House', while Paddy's was 'This is my island in the sun'.

With four young boys, home life could seem quite chaotic. With a gap of several years between the two sets of brothers, they paired off together. Yet there was intense rivalry between Stephen and Paul. Paul once came running into the house from the garden, crying bitterly because he would never be as old as Stephen. The two older brothers knew their younger ones as 'the babies'. They would argue vociferously, no holds barred, at any time, a spectacle which startled some guests. There were games of football in the garden or cycle races with home-made jumps. Every year there were big parties in the garden on Bonfire Night, with massive boxes of fireworks. Christmas was a huge occasion. The boys were always given a torch, a set of dominoes and a football each. Goalposts were set up in the house on Christmas morning. There was always a lot of laughter and a lot of noise. There were dogs, including Prince and Digby, an Old English Sheepdog. The boys had toy guns which filled the hall of the house with spent plastic pellets, no matter how hard their mother tried to clean up after them. She would buy them sweets in bulk from the local cash and carry, including Mars Bars and Maltesers. The boys, in Paddy's words, 'had a season ticket for the local accident and emergency', with split heads or broken arms. There would be occasional picnics, consisting of a flask of tea, boiled eggs, and, as a treat, salmon paste sandwiches. Another treat was apple sandwiches, with slices of apple topped with a sprinkling of sugar.

For Stephen Cronin, his father was 'my hero, always my hero, although he was quite often not there'. But 'when he was there, he gave an immense amount of love'. Paul too remembered how hard his father worked but 'when he was there, there was always some fun stuff to do'. For Philip, his childhood was 'sugar-coated'. He took his father's absences for granted for he knew nothing else. The younger boys, 'the babies', always felt that they saw their father in a different light from their elder brothers. While Stephen and Paul grew up through the boom, Philip and Paddy were teenagers in the aftermath of the cancelled *Daily Mirror* contract, when the golden years had passed and times were harder. Stephen and Paul, they felt, saw their father as omnipotent, which indeed he had been, while they developed a healthy respect for him from working alongside him in the business. Paul, on reflection, appreciates that 'we did grow up in a different time'.

Although the business was expanding rapidly as the boys were growing up, Frank did try to make time for the family. 'The family was always a major thing for me, and input from dad was important.' The one occasion when the boys could nearly always be guaranteed their father would be with them was on their Easter holiday which for years they took at Camp de Mar in Majorca. Later the family would buy two apartments in Los Cristianos in Tenerife which are still shared amongst them all. There was usually a summer holiday as well. 'Holidays were the biggest time with Dad,' remembered Stephen. Just occasionally holidays came second to Frank's work. Paul remembered how his father was usually happy for his mother to make all the decisions – 'but if it was something that was really important to him, it was his decision, and sometimes this got up Mum's nose, because ... there was just no give on his part at all.' Teresa was furious when Frank once cancelled a much-anticipated family holiday. Determined to go away, she made a last-minute booking for the Hotel Negresco in Nice, taking the two eldest boys with her.

All four boys went away to school. Stephen and Paul were sent away to prep school at Ampleforth, the leading Catholic independent school, where they later joined the senior school. Philip spent only a term at prep school before coming back home where his mother missed him. He returned to Ampleforth at the age of 13 where Paddy later joined him at the same age. The boys had mixed experiences at Ampleforth, with Paul and Paddy hating it. Paul forever associated the tune which heralded the Sunday evening radio programme, *Sing Something Simple,* with the misery of returning to school at the end of the weekend. His father thought nothing of driving to and from Ampleforth on a Saturday and again on a Sunday, six hours of driving on many weekends.

Teresa realised the enormity of the decision to send them away only when Stephen joined the senior school. She would be welcome, said the headmaster, to collect him again in 13 weeks' time. Seeing the look of absolute horror on her face, Frank began thinking how this challenge could be overcome. He had seen a nearby farm for sale, high up above sea level, close to the village of Wass, with views over the North York Moors and the Vale of York. Buying the farm, they decided to build a new house on the site. Frank and Teresa were discussing the idea as they drove through the village of Sutton under Whitestonecliff. Teresa conceded that Frank could have any sort of house he liked, 'so long,' she said, 'as it looks like that one,' pointing towards a house in the village. Frank stopped the car, knocked on the door of the house, and asked if the householder knew who had built it. He did and Frank employed the same man to build his new house. When Stephen and Paul were first taken to see the farm, it was a very wet night, and there was little to see. Building work had started and the two boys stood in the footings, already laying claim to their own rooms. Frank made sure that the boys' bedrooms, with a large bathroom, were at the opposite end of the house from the master bedroom.

Once the house was finished, weekends were often spent at the farm when the boys were at school. Since the boys were allowed out of school for country walks at the weekend, they and their friends could walk the mile to the farm and spend the afternoon there before going back. Frank, though, was never at the farm as often as Teresa, preoccupied as he was by business. Paul recalled how 'Mum adored Dad but often found him very frustrating because he was so focused on work'. Frank could often become so preoccupied that he became oblivious to any impact on other people. Sometimes when the family was travelling back north from the farm, Frank, who liked to think he was a bit of a farmer, and always watched *Farming Outlook* on Sundays, would stop for a chat at the house of a local farmer, leaving everyone else waiting in the car for a couple of hours. Frank would eventually build up a smallholding of 140 acres, with sheep and mixed crops, managed for him by a local farm manager. Frank came to value the house as a weekend retreat. Like Teresa, he resented the idea that parents should have no contact with their sons for such a long period at such an impressionable age. 'The principle of parental input was vital. I believed they should learn love and how to behave and other things like that from their parents.' In an idyllic situation, the farm is still well used by the family. As far as Frank was concerned, 'I will never regret buying that place' – it helped to give continuity to family life while the boys were at boarding school.

As a lifelong fan of Sunderland Football Club, Frank made the effort to take the boys regularly to matches. Every season he took a row of seats in the Clock Stand at Roker Park. His involvement with the club took an unexpected turn towards the end of 1976 when Frank received a visit in the old mill in Wilson Street from three of the club's directors. Football was very different in the days before the game was flooded with money from television and other commercial activities. The three were the chairman, Keith Collings, who ran the Luxdon Laundry business, Jack Ditchburn, a local solicitor, and Ted Evans, who managed his own construction company. Frank recounts the story. 'One day up these four steps came these three guys. And they said to me, "Frank, will you pay the wages?" And I said, "What bloody wages?" They said, "The players' wages." "Why would I want to pay the players' wages?" "Well, it's like this, Frank. We haven't got any money, the bank won't give us any money, and the players won't play on Saturday unless we pay them their wages." I said to them, "Well, you're gonna be surprised at my answer. I love the town and the football club's a large part of it. So, yes, I will. The rules are – there'll be one bank account, one cheque book and one signatory. If you don't want it, bugger off!" They had a two- minute conversation, came back and said "OK".'

The club had experienced financial troubles before. In 1957, the year before Sunderland were relegated from the first division after 68 consecutive seasons, the chairman, Bill Ditchburn, (Jack's father) and several directors were suspended following illicit payments to players. The club only returned to the first division in 1976 under Bob Stokoe, who had already taken them to their second FA Cup win in 1973. But consistent success would prove elusive for the next 20 years. The veneer of success in the mid-1970s masked serious financial shortcomings and the club was clearly on the brink of financial collapse before the deputation of directors met Frank Cronin. He was baffled by their predicament. 'How on earth do you win the cup in '73 and you go bust in '76? They must have been absolute idiots. I was dumbstruck. Here were three of the top guys in the town stood at my door saying they had no money to the run the business.' It was obvious why they called on him when they found themselves out of their financial depth. He was one of the town's most successful and prosperous businessmen, with a lifelong love of the club and the game. His immediate offer in response to the plea for help showed how deeply he cared about the future of the club. 'As a Sunderland lad, born and bred in the town, proud of Sunderland, Sunderland Football Club was an important part of the town and I've always wanted the club to do well.'

For the next six years the financial affairs of the club were effectively in the hands of Frank Cronin. 'I ran the club.' It is not too much to suggest that without his involvement, Sunderland would have struggled to survive. Nursing the club back to financial health took Frank a few hours every week. He had no more time to spare, running an expanding business with several hundred employees. Every Wednesday afternoon a clerk would come over from the club with the mail, bills and cheques, and Frank would authorise purchases and sign cheques. His own bank manager agreed without hesitation that Frank could open a completely separate account on behalf of the club. And there was just one account, one cheque book and one signatory. Although Frank was strictly in charge of finance, he was a de facto chairman. 'I didn't want to be chairman but I was absolutely in charge because [the other directors] couldn't do a thing.' He was often asked for his views on the club but deliberately kept a low profile with the press and the fans. The club's finances were helped when it returned to the first division during Frank's time on the board, and he was always involved in setting gate prices every year. He increased revenue from perimeter advertising, added paid-for executive boxes, introduced improved bonuses for wins, banned the use of the free bar in the board room except on match days and generally tightened up the club's financial controls. Although he knew the impact on the gate that a new star signing could have, he always asked the club manager, with whom he dealt directly, to justify any signing he had in mind. As a result, the club made three record signings, two under Ken Knighton in 1979, the third under Alan Durban in 1981, although with mixed results. The first was Stan Cummins, just 20 years old when the club paid a record £300,000 for him in November 1979. He proved to be a success during his four-year contract with the club, developing the knack of scoring goals at crucial moments. The second was the 25-year-old Argentine Claudio Marangoni, signed for £320,000 in December 1979. Despite his talent, he found it impossible to settle into English football and scored just three goals before he left the club a year later. The club paid £400,000 for the 18-year-old Ally McCoist in the summer of 1981. He too was disappointing during his two years with Sunderland. He scored just 8 goals in 56 appearances before moving to Glasgow Rangers where he achieved greater things. Frank later recalled that 'All three of my big signings were class. [The managers] were telling me the honest truth as far as they were concerned and they knew the decision was mine. And I would tell them to go and haggle before they came back and we did a deal.'

When Frank left the club, he handed over an account containing in excess of £600,000. 'It was for the team and the town.' Yet Frank's contribution to the club has been under-appreciated. Partly this was because of the low public profile he maintained. Keith Collings continued as chairman until he was succeeded by Tom Cowie in 1980. Frank had introduced Cowie to the club in the belief that as another very successful businessman he could help to bring financial stability to the club. Perhaps the lack of recognition is also because the club's success in climbing out of debt was not mirrored by its exploits on the pitch. His friends say that in the early 1980s Frank became disillusioned with the club for a variety of reasons, which coincided with difficulties at Edward Thompson, and he did not regret his eventual departure in 1982.

Edward Thompson continued to print match programmes and the club magazine free of charge for many years and Frank continued to take his family to games but it was only relatively recently that rifts dating back to the 1980s were finally healed. And in 1997 the club's new stadium, the Stadium of Light, was built just a five-minute walk away from the Edward Thompson factory. Frank likes to say that 'I walked away without a penny but they were very, very kind to me, because they moved the football stadium right next to my factory so I could walk there'.

As the boys grew older, their father always encouraged them to visit and later work in the factory. The boys were always made to feel welcome and never regarded as irritants. Philip always felt at home, particularly in the office, where Madge Johnson helped him with his first bank account. The boys were often in the factory during school holidays, with Philip's love of squash giving him another reason to come in. He remembered how 'the company was heaving, with people everywhere, it was very industrious'.

Frank played squash with Philip regularly from about the age of ten and would often take him along to squash competitions. Squash was Frank's premier pastime. According to his great rival and friend, Neil Wright, Frank advised a game of squash as the cure for everything. A game of squash on his own court was one of the few things which would make him late for an appointment. He enjoyed playing tennis too, playing doubles in the county championships with Tom Macdonald, Teresa's second cousin, but he was a much better squash player. He achieved league success with teams at town and county level. He also formed a company team, in which he usually alternated in the number-one slot with Micky Amer, and set up the Edward Thompson league. Neil Wright, who was Durham County's leading player for many years, described Frank as a player of 'flamboyant style'. He would never give up and was always chasing the ball. Although Neil always tried to stay out of the way of Frank's swinging racquet, he usually suffered bruises before the end of the game. On one occasion he even had Frank's teeth marks in his head. Frank still plays squash today at the age of

77, often against his grandchildren, although he rations the time he spends on court. He continues to relish the challenge, deploying against much younger opponents all the skills and strategies acquired in more than six decades of playing the game.

Philip had been interested in business from an early age. A toy cash register was one of his favourite toys. He began work experience in the factory when he was 14 and from the age of 15 or 16 began discussing with his father when he might join the business. His two elder brothers were already studying medicine – Stephen would become a leading consultant paediatrician and Paul a successful cosmetic physician – and Frank must have seen Philip in much the way his own father had seen him. When Philip worked at the company during his gap year, Frank involved him in everything he did, from major meetings to sales trips. When he went to university, he took his father's advice, taking a course in computing and electronics. Frank believed he should acquire a skill, believing management was an impossible subject to teach. When he graduated, his father made him assistant managing director at the tender age of 22, and three years later, when Frank took over as chairman of the area health authority, Philip became joint managing director.

The appointment to the health authority came out of the blue. One day Frank received a telephone call from Sir Bernard Tomlinson, a distinguished clinician and then chairman of the regional health authority. Tomlinson spent ten minutes persuading Frank to take over the chair of the area health authority. Frank protested. 'Come on! I'm a printer and paper maker!' Tomlinson, though, was not to be denied, telling Frank, 'I know exactly what I'm doing. I've done my homework'. The term was only for two years and Frank was eager to make an impact. He discovered that an organisation employing nearly 4,000 people lacked a rule book. With his secretary, Pat, he sat down to draw one up. The list became the patients' charter, introduced in Sunderland in April 1991, before the government's national scheme was launched. Copied on to large laminated sheets, it was displayed in all the hospital wards and GP surgeries in the authority. But Frank found instigating change in such a large organisation desperately hard, with much entrenched resistance. Despite this, he became a passionate supporter of the NHS, hugely impressed by the commitment of doctors and nurses, and remains so to this day. 'I still believe that the health service is brilliant, it is a fantastic way of achieving equality at a health level, and that is absolutely brilliant. And it would be a shame if that was changed in any way, it would be wrong.' He only served one term, perhaps failing to be re-appointed because of his forthright opinions.

When Frank returned to the business, he kept to the promise he had made to Philip that he would give up the role of managing director at the age of 60. By this time Paddy too was in the business. Paddy had considered medicine or the veterinary profession as a career after university, where he had studied biochemistry and physiology, and never really intended to join Edward Thompson. But he too had latent entrepreneurial leanings, identifying a gap in the clothing market in St Andrews, his university town, where he was keen to open a shop and take advantage of the opportunity. Instead, his father persuaded him that he needed a couple of years' experience in business, and he joined the company. The opportunity, of course, was seized by others.

Frank was absolutely delighted that two of his sons wanted to work in the company. 'I think the last thing in the world you should do is to try and encourage or discourage. It has to be their choice but if they want to come you should welcome them with open arms … Once they say they want to be in, you should be as smug as hell and say nowt.'

Philip was always ambitious for the business, driven and focused. As it turned out, Philip and his father failed to agree about the future of the paper mill, which led to Philip's departure in 1993. He was away several years, setting up his own business, Intermedia. This left Paddy, who had developed an affinity for the business, working alongside his father. The assumption was that Philip would return to take over the business, and he did come back to run the business as chief executive from 2002. But disagreements and differences over strategy and succession led him to conclude that he should concentrate on the development of his own on-line business and he left again in 2007. Frank had finally given up the reins in 2003, partly to look after Teresa, who had been diagnosed with lung cancer. Paddy has since run the business, although he is not the sole shareholder, as his father and grandfather had been in the past, with the shares spread across the four boys. Paddy was determined that the business, which had come through a difficult time, should survive and prosper. Like his father, he came to believe that Edward Thompson was more than the sum of its parts, and that business was about more than just making money – 'it's about the community, it's about the entity itself'.

Teresa Cronin died on 11 January 2004, less than a year after being formally diagnosed. Frank had looked after her with complete devotion and was utterly disorientated by her loss. He still drives Teresa's Jaguar for sentimental reasons. They had one each, both with personal number plates. Just as Teresa had thought Frank should have been addressed as Mr Cronin by his staff, so she thought he should have bought himself a Rolls-Royce. Frank, on the other hand, was happy being Frank and running Jaguars. He will always miss her. 'She's a hell of a miss ... you gradually, very, very gradually adjust ... what I try to avoid is self-pity which is counter-productive ..... you can't go charging into [the boys'] lives too much, you've got to sit back ... they're all in their prime and they know what they're doing.' He realises he must stand back and let his sons get on with their own lives. He still signs cheques for the company, as his father used to do, which keeps him interested. 'It helps to keep me involved without interfering.'

The stress of Teresa's death may have contributed towards Frank's diagnosis with Alzheimer's disease. He confesses that he was 'hacked off' when he was first told but has now become much more accepting and rarely talks about it. 'I am not worried about it now. It's part of ageing, of getting old, of not being able to play as many games of squash at a time.'

As well as squash, Frank still keeps up many of his other interests in retirement. His love of music has been lifelong. The boys all knew his fondness for Gilbert & Sullivan because whenever there was a family argument Frank would frequently break into song as a diversion. He became a karaoke fan thanks to a gift from Teresa. Often at a loss to know what to buy the man who never wanted anything other than a new squash racquet, she bought him a cheap karaoke machine one year as part of his Christmas presents. (Although he was always very generous, Frank could never see the point of giving presents. Teresa never wanted for anything, remembered Stephen, but little ever came from Frank as a gift.) Frank liked the karaoke machine so much that Teresa then bought a much better version. This was in spite of the fact that she considered such machines unsightly clutter. When Frank had acquired a quadraphonic audio system, Teresa insisted the speakers were housed in white cupboards with lace fronts, and covered the surface of the system with knick-knacks which always shook whenever the volume was turned up. Frank fell in love with karaoke. He hosts regular karaoke nights at his home, sometimes with as many as 50 people. His current machine has 1,700 indexed tracks. Although Frank has never been very comfortable with the latest technology, which sometimes means he has difficulty programming the machine, this has never been a hindrance, for he knows virtually every track off by heart. With his gift for mimicry, he can deliver 'Sweet Caroline' as if Neil Diamond himself was holding the microphone.

He still has an interest in the Variety Club of Great Britain, a charity which has been close to his heart for many years. 'It was,' said Frank, 'a big part of my life.' He was just 31 years old when he joined. He came into the Club because of his links with the showmen who were moving into bingo. Even though this was a time when the business was expanding rapidly, Frank still had more than enough energy to devote to the Club. He was regional chairman before he was 40 and, approaching his involvement as he did his work, injected a new vitality into the Club's activities. In the late 1970s, for instance, he gathered a team of Radio 1 DJs to play against Sunderland at Roker Park. For many years the company did the printing for the regional organisation free of charge. All this was part of his competitive outlook – he wanted the north-east region to be the best in the country. He would become regional chairman three times and also served as national chairman in 1981-82. He received a Silver Heart from Prince Charles in the 1980s (after Teresa was introduced to the Prince, who enquired where she was from, she tried to teach him to speak Geordie). In 2004 his commitment was recognised by an award and citation marking 40 years of service at the annual convention of Variety Club International. This award, for Frank, was 'the biggy'. He joked that he was so dedicated to the Club that at one charity auction he paid a thousand pounds for a Newcastle United shirt –- although he immediately gave it back so it could be sold again. He was proud that the Northern Region raised £250,000 annually during his last three years as chairman. According to Neil Wright, 'Frank Cronin *is* the Variety Club in the north-east, full stop.'

Frank found the work of the charity in helping disadvantaged and disabled children 'terribly motivational'. 'You can,' he said, 'make things a little bit better.' As well as his organisational role, Frank was always happy to take an active part in fund-raising. After the Golden Hearts appeal was initiated in 1991, he was determined that the north-east region would lead the way in raising funds. He realised that the key lay in effective distribution and he persuaded the Co-op and other supermarkets to sell the Hearts. Even today Frank can still be found collecting money with his colleagues in supermarkets and other locations. He always acknowledged that whatever he achieved on the Club's behalf could not have happened without other people. 'I was in a much better position to be successful because I had this team of helpers. It was not a Frank Cronin effort, it was a team effort.'

On behalf of the Club, Frank used his fund-raising skills to extend the Sunshine Coaches scheme throughout the region, which now operates some 150 coaches. He always visited every school which received a coach, talking with the children and teachers, which gave him huge personal satisfaction. Ever practical, Frank made a point of ensuring that organisations which were given a new coach always had somewhere to keep them under cover so they would last two or three years longer. (Today his secretary Pat, whom Frank involved in the Club, now chairs the regional Sunshine Coaches section.) He has been typically unafraid of making his views known. When the national organisation was considering stipulating a minimum fund-raising commitment from schools before they could receive a grant, Frank spoke strongly against the idea, pointing out that for some schools raising any more at all would be a great achievement.

How much Frank cares about the causes supported by the Club comes through in how he talks about a visit he and his friend Jim Cleghorn made to present a special bicycle to a young autistic boy and his mother in their third- floor flat in Seaham. Frank was deeply concerned to make sure that he connected with the boy. He immediately began talking to him at his own level, directly and without condescension, patiently waiting for the boy to respond. 'I told him, "My name is Frank. You've got to remember that so when I come here with your bike you've got to say, 'Thank you, Frank'. What have you got to say?" "Thank you, Frank." And all of a sudden the bike is real to the kid a little bit more. This is the guy that's going to bring it and all of a sudden I'm important. Once you've got him, it's easy. And you say all the right things to him, all the good things you can possibly say, you say, and mum glows. It's got more effect on mum than on the little one, and you've got both of them.' Today Frank still runs the Club's South of the Tyne committee from his home.

When a member of staff, Norman Howe, having an autistic son himself, set up Education and Services for People with Autism (ESPA), Frank was keen to help, as support from the Variety Club ended when a young person reached 19. Frank has helped to fund an eight-berth caravan at Wooler where carers and their children could have a break. When Frank went up for the hand-over, he struck up a rapport with one young man named Stephen when he discovered that they shared the same name. 'And at the end I went up to him and shook his hand and said, "Lovely to have met you, Stephen, I hope you have a very happy time." And he said, "Thank you, I hope you are happy too, Francis Stephen".'

Frank also relishes being a Lloyd's name. He and Teresa invested a modest sum in Lloyd's in 1982 from the proceeds of Edward Thompson International. Frank's initial investment has grown considerably over the years and today, as a member of the High Premium Group, he underwrites several million pounds of risk and travels regularly to London for meetings. His involvement also led to his participation in a members' racing syndicate which owns a horse named 'Lutine Charlie', which has had modest success.

Frank gains great joy from his grandchildren. Stephen and his wife Suzanne, who married in 1986, have three children – Alex, born in 1987, Sophie, born in 1988 and Benedick, born in 1993. Paul was married firstly to Ravi Pawa in 1986 and secondly to Jane McDean in 2004 and has two daughters, Francesca, born in 1991, and Bethany, born in 1994. Philip married Alison Gourley in 1986. They had been born four weeks apart and one street away from each other and their mothers knew each other well. The twins, Michael and James, were born in 1989, and Robert was born in 1992. Paddy married Morven MacKean in 1990 and they have two children, Fionn, born in 1997, and Molly, born in 1999. As Frank tells you that half of them are currently at university, he adds, 'I still think that's fantastic'. Being a grandfather, he says, is 'fantastic, absolutely fantastic. They're all lovely. It's wonderful to have them. The biggest joy in life is children. Even at 77, when you're getting ready for the last round, or whatever you might call it, it's a tremendous joy. And they don't see you as old, they'll help you but they don't see you as old. They'll ring up and ask for a game of squash.'

He also has a group of close friends whom he often entertains and with whom he often goes out, learning to enjoy being out in company without Teresa. Still an imposing figure, with a dashing charm, and an impish twinkle in his eye, he has not lost the capacity to captivate those he meets.

Paddy speaks for all the boys when he talks of his 'warm and soft and friendly and forgiving home, very supportive, happy, giggly and safe'. The boys never wanted for affection, attention or advice. Stephen remembered being very upset when boys at school told him he would come to hate his father – he never would and he never has. From his father Stephen learned in particular the importance of openness and honesty. He has never forgotten one incident from his schooldays. He had driven himself back to school but when his housemaster asked him who had dropped him off, he said his father had. When he later told his father this, Frank insisted that Stephen should return to his housemaster and tell the truth. He also had the knack, Stephen said, of gently bringing you round to his point of view. When Stephen took it into his head that he wanted to buy a former London taxi, his father did not tell him it was a ridiculous idea. But he just worked into the conversation enough of the disadvantages in such a way that Stephen quickly discarded the idea. Paul discovered how his father respected the achievements which came with hard work. When he was 19, Paul had saved up enough money to take a flying course, but he wanted to ask his father's permission. When he told his father what he wanted to do, Frank told him that he would not pay towards it. But when Paul told him that all he wanted was his consent, his father simply paused and then said, 'Well, make sure you don't kill yourself'. Frank reasoned that Paul had earned his money and he could do with it what he liked. After Paul passed, Frank was his first – and nervous – passenger. Paul took him on a flight over the house at Cleadon, tipping the wing of the plane as they passed over. Frank would later tell friends, 'I went for a flight with my son the other day and it was perfectly OK ... but where was the pilot?' Paul also learned from his father the importance of following whatever drives you through life. So, for instance, Paul flew a paramotor over 2,000 miles of the UK during 20 days in August 2010 to raise money for a local hospital. He also learned from his father that everyone makes mistakes but you should never worry about them. At home Philip believed he could not have had a better upbringing, with a father he regarded as invincible and a loving mother. In business Philip had watched his father with awe, he was so quick, so confident, with an incredible grasp of detail, the king of the business.

When Frank Cronin talks about his life, a recurring theme is his firm belief in the power of love in its widest sense. Combined with his ceaseless optimism, this has proved a potent force. He did not have an easy childhood but he and his brothers were brought up in a loving home. Frank and Teresa, who enjoyed a long and loving marriage, made sure that their four sons were brought up in the same loving atmosphere. Frank applied the same principle to his business life, with employees, customers and suppliers. It helped to create a business which remains the world's largest printer of bingo tickets but perhaps more importantly for Frank it provided a living to thousands of families over more than half a century. 'Love Thy Neighbour' has also driven his commitment to the Variety Club and his other charitable interests. And today it underpins his relationship with his many grandchildren. There can be few more valuable lessons in life.

INDEX